Jangar

The publisher and the University of California Press Foundation gratefully acknowledge the generous support of the Constance and William Withey Endowment Fund in History and Music.

Jangar

The Heroic Epic of the Kalmyk Nomads

———

Translated by

Saglar Bougdaeva

UNIVERSITY OF CALIFORNIA PRESS

University of California Press
Oakland, California

Library of Congress Cataloging-in-Publication Data

Names: Bougdaeva, Saglar, 1972- translator.
Title: Jangar : the heroic epic of the Kalmyk nomads / translated by Saglar
    Bougdaeva.
Other titles: Jangɣr. English.
Description: Oakland, California : University of California Press, [2022] |
    Includes bibliographical references.
Identifiers: LCCN 2022008255 (print) | LCCN 2022008256 (ebook) |
    ISBN 9780520344723 (paperback) | ISBN 9780520975651 (ebook)
Subjects: LCSH: Epic poetry, Kalmyk.
Classification: LCC PL430.9.D88 E5 2022 (print) | LCC PL430.9.D88 (ebook) |
    DDC 894/.2—dc23/eng/20220720
LC record available at https://lccn.loc.gov/2022008255
LC ebook record available at https://lccn.loc.gov/2022008256

Manufactured in the United States of America

31   30   29   28   27   26   25   24   23   22
10   9   8   7   6   5   4   3   2   1

To my father, Ilya,
Bougda's grandson,
Erdni's son,
Hero Dogzma's descendant,
the Chair of the Supreme Council
of the Republic of Kalmykia

According to the history
Of the Tuoba Wei dynasty (386–534),
The Xianbei Mongolian-speaking nomads
Were led into China by a flying horse spirit
That bellowed like an ox.
The Kalmyks called the spirit
Ki-Moren, the Wind-Horse,
And kept the image on their banners.

CONTENTS

LIST OF ILLUSTRATIONS

All illustrations by Delia Dunbar

Introduction

This translation presents for the first time in English the epic treasure of the Kalmyk nomads, *Jangar*. As nomadic artists of the Great Eurasian Steppe, Kalmyks have witnessed, memorized, and orally transmitted some of the greatest transformations, both victorious and tragic, in the history of civilizations. The significance of their art for the world literary heritage can hardly be overstated.

Kalmyk means "the remained"; they are the remaining Mongols of Genghis Khan's empire in Europe. Today, Kalmyks still live in the territory that was once the Golden Horde, founded by Juchi, one of the sons of Genghis Khan, near the site of its capital, Sarai. Sarai, with its magnificent architecture, has long been covered by the sands of time inside the hills of the Great Steppe. But the Kalmyk nomads have managed to preserve the great treasure of their heritage, carefully transmitting their epic narrative across generations. The most vivid work of the Kalmyk people, the heroic model for life and death that has always inflamed hearts and incited tears, is the grand epic *Jangar*.

Jangar belongs to a genre of oral literature about extraordinary deeds from the heroic age. The basis of its creation is the unification of individual songs that are not connected by an overall plot but rather evolve around a central axis, the Bumba union of seventy kingdoms. In every song, a hero begins and ends his adventure in the Bumba banquet hall with drinking, feasting, and merrymaking. This cyclization reflects the Kalmyk collective processes in which the epic becomes

1

the cycle of life outside the perception of time, simultaneously the epic past, and a nonlinear projection into the future.

Jangar sings a tribute to the heroic deeds of the protectors of the Bumba union. The Bumba world of nomadic heroes is a world of centaurs, not in their physical form, but in an imagined united identity. When a hero is born, his heroic horse is born too. Together they recover from misfortunes and triumph in adventures. All heroes, humans and horses, share a passionate dedication to the Bumba union, as reflected in their oath:

> We throw our lives to the edge of the spears,
> Devote our passion to the Bumba completely,
> Strip our torsos and rip out our hearts,
> To the people we give our blood to the end.
>
> (Lipkin 1940, chap. 11)

As is typical of a heroic epic, in *Jangar* the days are compressed until the moment of heroic deed, when the hours become stretched. The heroes belong to a common treasury of culturally recognizable characters, each a model for a specific trait: Scarlet Lion Khongor for bravery, Shaman Golden Heart for wisdom, Handsome Mingian for sophistication, Serious Sanal for contemplation, Mediator Jilgan for diplomacy. Heroes' names are determined by the moment of their heroic deed. For example, Scarlet Lion Khongor, outwardly shy, is the bravest man in the universe: a roaring lion sleeps in his rib cage. When the moment comes for him to protect the Bumba union, Khongor transforms into a fearless lion. Khongor is also associated with different shades of red; in his heroic moments, his lion spirit shines with ecstatic scarlet sunbeams. Even in everyday life, Khongor is recognized from afar by his radiant red hair, which despite his grooming attempts look like a lion's mane.

The name Jangar (also transliterated as Zangar) is given to the heroes' legitimate leader and to the epic itself; its cultural meaning should not be underestimated. Scarlet Lion Khongor and Jangar are equals in their oath to protect the Bumba union. But what makes Jangar, rather than Khongor, a leader among all the scions of competing families is his virtuous character. Jangar's name denotes one who lives "by ethics" or "by honor" and reflects his call to lead. Living by honor is what holds the union of equal kingdoms together and makes it invincible. *Jangar* as a concept links individual heroic deeds to a united destiny, to a community of honor and justice.

The *Jangar* epic varies in length based on the training of *Jangar* singers (*jangarchi*) and is usually transmitted by singing. The training of *jangarchi* Eelian Ovla (ten songs, 6,049 lines) and that of *jangarchi* Mukebyun Basangov (six songs, 5,803 lines) reflect the most prominent traditions of the Kalmyk epic. This translation is based on ten *Jangar* songs performed by the famed Kalmyk rhapsodist Eelian Ovla (1857–1920), who was born into a line of *jangarchi* stretching back over centuries. The epic is characterized by alliteration derived from a rich poetic tradition with prehistoric roots. Though not captured in this translation, in the Kalmyk, the stress falls on the initial sound, which is repeated in every line of the verse:

> Sovereign Khan Jangar
> Striking with his looks like a moon
> Silk woven robes were chosen for him
> Stitched by selected highborn queens
> Sewn only by his wife.
> Sixteen-year-old Khatun, armed with her scissors,
> Signature robes of hers made only for her loving Khan.

Yet *Jangar* is not just a song; it is a passionate performance. The cycles, or episodes, are performed as a sung recitative in a structured way and accompanied by a musical instrument such as the two-stringed *dombra*, the three- or four-stringed *tovshur*, or the violin-like *biiv*. Eelian Ovla played the *dombra* and could sing multiple cycles in rapid succession, captivating his audience for an entire night.

All episodes begin with the same prologue song, which recapitulates the creation of the Bumba union and its protectors. Each episode focuses on one protector and his heroic deed. Eelian's favorite episode was about Serious Sanal, whose name denotes a person who contemplates or philosophizes. Before singing this episode, Eelian would fire up his audience: "Are you ready? Shall we send Serious Sanal, the son of Bulingir, on his glorious journey?" Their emotions running high, his listeners would often cry out or jump from their seats and throw their hats on the ground during particularly dramatic parts of the performance.

We learn about the ritual of *Jangar*'s performance in the epic itself, when Princess Gerenzel falls in love with Khongor and invites him to sing about the Bumba heroes at a banquet. The extravagant party is thrown by her suitor Wrestler Tsagan, who arrives with five hundred knights, a show of force meant to remind the public of his engagement to the princess. Khongor sings until the first light of dawn, and the princess's glass palace, designed in the shape of an eagle, trembles from his energized voice. Khongor's masterful performance is rewarded in the morning, when he receives a thousand yellow-headed sheep. In real life, performances of *Jangar* were in high demand, and master *jangarchi* enjoyed elevated social status. Noble Kalmyk families were responsible for the financial support and organization of both private and public performances of *Jangar*.

It is important to note that the epic's oral transmission does not imply that the nomadic audience was illiterate. Up until the destruction of the Kalmyk Khanate in 1771, Kalmyks observed laws that promoted literacy among all rich and poor men. In fact, Kalmyk public education laws and practices were not only well codified, but also more advanced than comparable laws of other states. For example, the 1640 Civil Code of Criminal Laws, or Tsaajin Bichig (*tsaajin* means "criminal" and *bichig* denotes a written document) stated that if the sons of nobles were not attentive to reading and writing, a fine equal to the price of a three-year-old camel would be levied against the father. In addition, commoners were required to teach their sons reading and writing commensurate with opportunity and ability. Nobles assumed their own educational expenses, and any collected fines were distributed to cover the educational needs of the poor. Thus, *Jangar* was not a primitive oral tradition for illiterate nomads. It was a live artistic form that produced, rather than a static artifact, an ephemeral transmission of literary creation suitable to nomadic settings.

Following centuries of oral transmission, a written version of *Jangar* would become the Kalmyks' national literary monument. In 1908, during fieldwork in Kalmykia, Nomto Ochirov, a Kalmyk lawyer and philologist from St. Petersburg University, discovered Eelian Ovla, from whom he recorded ten songs (6,049 lines) that would form the basis of the first recorded and published version of *Jangar*. Nomto transcribed the songs using the original Kalmyk script and published the first print edition in St. Petersburg in 1910, establishing *Jangar* as a literary work. More importantly, when Nomto compiled a coherent body of ten cycles from the oral tradition, he successfully defended his theory that *Jangar* is not a collection of individual songs but indeed the Kalmyk national epic in its artistic entirety and completeness.

In 1940, Semyon Lipkin, a Russian literary translator, published a poetic adaptation for a wider Russian audience. Only a few years later, Stalin deported the entire Kalmyk population to Siberia and eliminated Kalmyk literature from the published world. Nomto Ochirov was himself arrested four times for his intellectual convictions and deported to settlements in Kazakhstan and Siberia.

That the heritage of the Kalmyks and other nomadic peoples has survived repressive regimes at all is thanks to the unequivocal commitment of people—Kalmyks, Russians, and others—who value the ancient voices of humanity. In spite of their efforts, Stalin's repressive orders silenced nomadic voices for almost a century, rendering them mute in the global discourse of world literature. *Jangar* is a principal conduit of nomadic cultural transmission, and reading it opens the imagination to the Great Steppe, its inhabitants, and their heroes.

HISTORICAL BACKGROUND

In medieval and early modern times, Kalmyks were known as Oirads. As stated in *Jangar,* the center of Oirad culture was Altai, the mountains of gold. According to the ancient classic *The Secret History of the Mongols* (written circa 1240), the Oirads' sociopolitical milieu dramatically changed in 1207, when Genghis Khan, recognizing the significance of the Oirad cultural heritage, married his two daughters to sons of the Oirad prince Khudukha-beki. The Oirads joined the army of Genghis Khan's son Juchi in his European expansion and the establishment of Juchi's kingdom on the Volga River.

In the thirteenth century, Ata-Malik Juvaini (1226–1283), a historian at the Mongol court of northern Persia, stressed the role of the Oirad (or Oirat) elite: "The Oirat are one of the best known of the Mongol tribes, and to that tribe belong most of the maternal uncles of the children and grand-children of Genghis Khan, the reason being that at the time of his first rise to power the Oirat came forward to support and assist him and vied with one another in their alacrity to tender allegiance, and in recognition of their services an edict was issued concerning that tribe to the effect that the daughters of their emirs should be married to the descendants of Genghis Khan" (Boyle 1958, 505).

Elevated by their imperial in-law status, the Oirad-Kalmyk political dynasties found a new calling in military and state-building leadership at the expanding western frontiers of the Mongolian empire.

After the fall of the dynasty of Mongols in China led by Genghis Khan's grandson Kublai Khan, the Oirads consolidated power under the talented commander Esen (1407–1455), who would lead them to dominate the Eurasian steppe road. The Oirads' last large territorial expansion took place in the seventeenth and eighteenth centuries, when their realm covered vast expanses of Inner Eurasia, from the Caspian Sea steppes in the west to Tibet in the east, and from the forests of Western Siberia to the oases in East Turkestan (now Xinjiang in China). Consequently, the last nomadic empire built by the Oirads played an important role in the historical fate of many peoples of Eastern Europe, the North Caucasus, and Central Asia.

The establishment of nomadic empires would have been impossible without the participation of heroic women. Historically, women played an integral role in the military and political affairs of nomadic polities. The Ottoman writer Evliya Çelebi (1611–1684), whose *Book of Travels* entered the canon of global literature, captured the era when border hostilities in Central Asia were at their peak. According to Çelebi, warriors from Tashkent, raiding the area bordering Kalmyk country, captured some Kalmyk nomads. Kalmyk warriors immediately chased down and fought the Tashkent raiders. After the battle, when armor and clothes were removed from the fallen Kalmyks, it was revealed that they were women.

Indeed, Kalmyk women were legendary both on the battleground and in government decision-making. Orghina Khatun, the granddaughter of the Oirad leader Khudukha-beki and Genghis Khan, had fiscal control over the rich Fergana Valley and ruled in Central Asia for almost a decade (1251–1260). Examples of women's autonomy echo throughout *Jangar*. For example, in cycle 2, the council of nobility accepts Princess Gerenzel's proposal to join Jangar's khanate when she takes the offspring of livestock as a wedding present:

> If our princess takes
> the livestock offspring
> To faraway lands,
> Animals will follow their offspring,

> Owners will follow their herds,
> Nomads will migrate to Jangar's Khanate.

In *Jangar*, Bumba as the union of kingdoms mirrors the confederation of the Oirad khanates. The strength of the Oirad union was especially marked in 1640, when the political elite from the Kalmyk Khanate on the Volga River, the Khoshut Khanate on Kokonor Lake, and the Jungar Khanate in the Altai Mountains gathered at a congress of the Oirad and Mongol political dynasties. The representatives discussed political unity and adopted the Civil Code of Criminal Laws, or Tsaajin Bichig.

The state builder of the Kalmyk Khanate, Ayuka Khan (1669–1724), seems to have exemplified the union of Oirad khanates through family coalitions and transcontinental migrations. Ayuka Khan was the progeny of a marriage between members of two familial dynasties from the Kalmyk and Jungar Khanates. As a child he traveled more than two thousand miles from the Kalmyk Khanate to the Jungar Khanate to live with his maternal grandfather, Batur Hun-tuichi, scion of the House of Choros (the Choros being the leading Oirad dynasty at the time). All Oirads considered the House of Choros and the legendary state-builders Khudukha-beki (thirteenth century), Esen (fifteenth century), and Batur Hun-tuichi (seventeenth century) to be of the sky with divine right in the process of political leadership and cultural transmission.

Batur Hun-tuichi's teachings about state building were not in vain. After Ayuka's return to the Volga River, the Kalmyk Khanate reached its peak under his leadership. By the 1680s, Ayuka had expanded the power and prestige of his khanate across the Eurasian steppe. When the Jungar Khanate was destroyed in 1758, many Jungar families under the House of Choros migrated to the Kalmyk Khanate, strengthening their family coalitions in the Volga region. Until the Russian Revolution in 1917, the descendants of Khudukha-beki, the Tundutov dynasty from the House of Choros, were the custodians of *Jangar* and other nomadic cultural and political traditions.

Today, despite the destruction of the Oirad union of khanates, the Jungar Khanate in 1758 and the Kalmyk Khanate in 1771, Kalmyks sustained, though with a different degree of success, their political autonomy, demographic balance, and culture. The Kalmyk national epic

Jangar is intertwined with the life of Kalmykia and its heroes. Even the life of Nomto Ochirov, who brought *Jangar* to the academic world, becomes a heroic introduction to *Jangar.* Nomto Ochirov's childhood name, Nokha, was associated with the animal spirit of a dog. By finding his calling and becoming a cultural model, he earned his heroic name, Nomto (scholar).

His father worked for the Tundutov family, and Nomto Ochirov was born in 1886 on the Tundutov estate. Princess Elzata (Ölzätä) raised both her son Danzan Tundutov (1888–1923) and her son's friend Nomto Ochirov in the epic tradition of *anda,* or sworn brotherhood friendship, represented by Jangar and Khongor. After completing their studies in St. Petersburg, the two young men were actively involved in the cultural and political affairs of Kalmykia. Like many Kalmyks, both fought on the side of the White Army in the Russian Civil War. Following a defeat by the Red Army in 1919, a small group of Kalmyk troops and their families managed to escape on French and British ships leaving Black Sea ports. The two friends would last meet in a port in Crimea. Prince Danzan boarded a ship while Nomto Ochirov stayed behind, pointing to his abandoned Kalmyk countrymen and saying, "If you are going to suffer, suffer with your people; if you are going to die, die with your people" (quoted from the short film " Prince Danzan Tundutov and Nomto Ochirov," directed by Mikhail Zakrevskij, written by Gennadij Korneev, and featuring Badma Pyurveev and Vyacheslav Khurgunov, "RIA – Kalmykia" and "TV Channel—Khamdan").

Prince Danzan Tundutov could not find peace in exile in Paris and returned to Russia in November 1922, where he was arrested by the GPU (a forerunner of the KGB) twice, upon his arrival and later, in April 1923. By the decision of the GPU court session on August 2, 1923, Prince Tundutov was sentenced to be shot. The decree was carried out on August 7, 1923. For many decades, until the corresponding archives were declassified, the place of execution and the place of burial remained unknown. Only recently a group of activists found that Prince Danzan Tundutov was killed outside Yauzskaya Hospital in Moscow. In his last letter before execution he wrote, "Those who know how to fight, know how to love and forgive" (E. Gerson, *NTV*, June 7, 2020, https://www.ntv.ru/video/1870880/; born in the EU, Pushkin's descendant submitted his documents for Russian citizenship).

Fortunately, Prince Danzan's family had remained in France. In 2020 Baron Serge Graevenitz, a descendant of the Tundutovs and of the family of Russian poet Alexander Pushkin, settled in Kalmykia and brought with him the flag of the Kalmyk emigrants in Europe. Nomto Ochirov's niece managed to preserve, through the Kalmyk deportations to Siberia in 1943, the flagpole topper of the House of Choros. The biographical accounts of scholar Nomto and prince Danzan highlight how, inspired by *Jangar* (which means one who lives by "ethics" and "honor"), Kalmyks repeat the scenes of friendship, love, and heroic adventures in their real lives.

NOMAD AESTHETIC

As performed across the Eurasian steppe, *Jangar* includes countless songs that represent the old boundaries of the union of Öirad khanates. They reflect the fate of the Oirad-speaking nomadic peoples who were consolidated in vast geographic and historical settings: the Kalmyk Oirads in today's Russia, the Western Mongol Oirads in today's Mongolia, the Xinxiang Oirads in today's China. To understand the epic scope of *Jangar,* one must consider nomadic sensibilities rather than modern national boundaries.

Jangar captivates us with its boundless sense of belonging. In the epic's conflicts, enemies are intentionally unidentifiable, as today's enemy may have been related to your family in the past crossroads of migration. Moreover, time as a linear concept is intentionally dropped from the narration. Thus, *Jangar* is a timeless reimagining of the collective lived experience of the nomads, and a model of united being.

Jangar extends its roots into many distant epochs. Trying to pinpoint the era of its creation will never enable us to understand its true depth, complexity, and power. It is not surprising that the duration of its existence is disputed. On the one hand, the official Soviet celebration of five hundred years of *Jangar* took place in 1940. This was based on Sergei Kozin's (1879–1956) hypothesis that the cyclization of the epic songs originated in the fifteenth century, when the Oirads reached the peak of their power under Esen.

On the other hand, Mikhail Gryaznov (1902–1984), whose archaeological discovery in 1929 of the Pazyryk early nomadic culture in the Altai Mountains attracted worldwide attention, highlighted an earlier period. Gryaznov argued that the heroic epic tradition of the region first originated in the third to first century BCE, evolving from generation to generation for more than two thousand years and coming down to the present as a modified oral transmission. Gryaznov emphasized that archaeological artifacts from that era included images consistent with *Jangar*'s heroic-age elements, creating a coherent system of intelligibility that allowed the nomadic carriers to mediate the world around them.

Of particular interest to Gryaznov were two bronze belt plaques from Ordos in Inner Mongolia. They depict a battle between two dismounted horsemen of the third to first century BCE. The images on the two plaques are identical in every detail: the number of leaves on the trees, the position of the horses, the arrangement of plaques on the horse harnesses. However, the two plaques are not a mechanical reproduction of the same image but handmade artifacts. The proportions and sizes of individual parts of the plaques do not exactly coincide, and one plaque is made as openwork, whereas the other is a solid plate. According to Gryaznov, these two artifacts were likely made at different times, in different places, and by different craftsmen. Thus, the depiction of the wrestling combat was not an isolated case, but an example of the type of socially significant theme that was reproduced repeatedly in a coherent system of cultural intelligibility.

The scene on the Ordos belt plaques is reflected in the description of the wrestling combat of heroes in *Jangar*:

> "Let's not torment our herbivorous friends.
> A shoulder against shoulder
> A chest against chest,
> Shall we try out our hero's power,
> a human gift from our mothers and fathers?"
>
> Two knights dismounted,
> Tying their horses to the saddlebows,
> They changed their attire.
> Togya rolled the kulan skin pants
> Above his knees.
> Lion Khongor rolled the deerskin pants
> Above his calves.

Here we see how the Oirads, through the collective use and circulation of formulaic tropes, preserved their canon of archaic rituals. The burden of sustaining the collective memory was not placed solely on the *Jangar* singers. Everyone, from the artists and craftsmen who created the belt plaques to the audience members who wore them, was familiar with these ritual tropes. In fact, *Jangar* brought no burden to the Kalmyk collective memory, but rather an uplifting lightness from shared sensibilities of honor, love, and vulnerability.

The wrestling depicted in the unearthed plaques and in *Jangar*'s narration reveals the degree to which the nomad aesthetic honors ritual: the wrestling match is divided into certain visual and sensual moments (stripping a muscular torso, putting on and rolling up soft scarlet pants, tying a silk sash) that intensify and slow the passage from mortal human to timeless hero on the verge of death. It is clear that for the Oirads it was important to follow the ritual of wearing and rolling up long pants before a wrestling combat. According to Gryaznov, this ritual was preserved among the Oirads but lost among the Mongols in Mongolia. (The change in ritual is documented in *The Secret History of the Mongols,* which notes that the famous wrestler Buri-Bokho wore a leather loincloth during the 1201 wrestling competition organized by Genghis Khan.)

From *Jangar* we know how to wear belts with plaques, how to show our status by wearing them, and how much such belts are worth:

> Over a gauzy undershirt
> And three fine silk robes
> He put on three layers of peacetime
> And unique battle armor
> Over the *ludang* silk,
> He fastened the iron belt
> Equal in cost to seventy horses.

Indeed, from a nomadic perspective, you are what you wear. The nomad aesthetic regarding belts, robes, pants, and boots has changed remarkably little over time. We can fast-forward from the Altai region in the third to first century BCE to Altai in the seventh to eighth century CE and find classic nomadic style intact. For example, in burial mounds in the Oirad autonomous oblast in Altai (the former territory of the Jungar Khanate), Soviet archaeologist Sergei Kiselev unearthed a fine inventory of the aristocratic strata of Altai society of the seventh and eighth centuries CE. The central figure in one of the burial mounds was a wealthy man. He was lying at the bottom of the excavated pit, stretched out, with his head to the north. Following Altai fashion, the man wore layers of fine silk robes, tightened with a silver belt made of sixty-five plaques. There were no pockets in the robes; three silk pouches were attached to his belt. A birch-bark quiver with Hunnu-type "whistling" arrows was also attached to the belt. The man's leather boots were elegantly fastened with buckles and straps around his ankles.

The Oirads' aesthetic survived their dramatic move in 1207 from Altai to the Golden Horde on the Volga River. A major find in excavations of Jukhta burial mounds in the Golden Horde that date to the thirteenth and fourteenth centuries CE was a noble mounted warrior attired in layers of silk robes, a belt with plaques, two pouches instead of pockets, and soft leather boots.

Nomads knew their silk. In *Jangar,* it is widely described as being used for robes, capes, palace decorations, and bedroom interiors. Silk was greatly appreciated not only for its sleek softness and elegance, but also for its incompatibility with the activity of body lice, considered the most dangerous pathogen at the time and blamed for epidemics of typhus and other infectious diseases.

In the thirteenth and fourteenth centuries, dramatic transcontinental migrations brought a novel development in the textile industry and introduced a new luxury commodity, *ludang:* "Over the *ludang* silk, he fastened the iron belt." *Ludang* silk was so significant that the term was added to *Jangar's* aesthetic canon. *Lu* means "dragon," and *dang* means "overall" or "throughout." The *ludang* textile from the Jukhta burial ground was silk woven with gold and covered with repeating images of roaring dragons hunting down helpless geese. It displays a harmonious synthesis of Persian, Chinese, and Central Asian styles, yet the predominant aesthetic is that of the Hunnu, the powerful confederation of nomadic peoples who glorified the spirit of animals and the laws of nature.

In today's Kalmykia, silk robes, belts with plaques, and soft leather boots are worn for traditional Kalmyk dances that draw a million views on YouTube. The popularity of Kalmyk culture can be attributed in part to Russian choreographer Igor Moiseyev (1906–2007), who despite Stalin's persecution of the Kalmyks dared to include their dance in his signature character dance repertoire. Of experiencing Kalmyk culture through dance, Moiseyev stated that "the spiritual wealth obtained through the arts and culture is the only thing that can be transmitted over time. This is what feeds people's souls. After death, people do not lose it, and in another epoch they are born with the spiritual wealth that they acquired earlier" (Korobkova 2016).

NOMADIC STATECRAFT

Jangar is rooted in the Great Eurasian Steppe and its nomadic empires. To understand the heroic-age statecraft depicted in *Jangar*, it is important to highlight its continuity with early nomadic multilingual polities in the regions of the Altai Mountains and the Yenisei River, particularly the Hunnu (Xiongnu) empire. By controlling the Great Steppe Route in the third to first century BCE, the Hunnu established a blueprint for successive nomadic empires. One among many such polities was the Oirad union of khanates, which used the Hunnu model in its political and cultural processes. The cultural ties and sensibilities reflected in *Jangar* were greatly influenced by the Hunnu statecraft and aesthetic, which was dominated by motifs of horses and archery.

The standard description of the Hunnu bureaucracy, which was divided into left and right wings, is given in the *Shi Ji* (*Records of the Grand Historian*) of Sima Qian (145–86 BCE):

> Under the *shanyu* there were
> *Tuichi* (Hunnu princely lineage) of the left and right wings,
> *Lu-li* (*Elu* familial lineage) of the left and right wings,
> Generals of the left and right wings,
> Commanders of the left and right wings,
> Household administrators of the left and right wings.

Through oral narration, Kalmyks have managed to preserve their archaic vocabulary, in particular, the state nomenclature used in early nomadic empires. *Shanyu* is an early old Oirad term combining *shan* ("state," or, in the archaic language, "exchequer") and *yu*[-*n*] (authority). Vowel harmony (soft or hard) is a foundational rule in the Mongolic languages. Following the soft harmony rule of reading, the word is *lu-li* pronounced as "elu-eli." Elu (or Yelu) was one of the most powerful dynasties in Inner Asia. *Eli* is a term for "elite."

Historically, nomadic polities in Inner Asia replaced the term *shanyu* with *khan* during the khanate of the Rourans (380–555 CE). It is important to note that Oirad leaders such as Batur Hun-tuichi preferred the political term *Hun-tuichi* (*Hun* denotes Hunnu and *tuichi* means prince) over *khan* (king). This preference signified their cultural continuity with the Hunnu nomadic empire. The translation of *Hun* in the Oirad dictionary of archaic words is "magnanimous." In the Hunnu tradition, state builders were expected to exude charisma, bear trouble calmly, disdain meanness and pettiness, and display a noble generosity. Thus, holders of the *Hun-tuichi* title were held to a very high standard in the Oirad political community.

As we learn from *Jangar,* for socially significant terms to endure, they must be simple. The original name for the Oirad homeland was Jungar. The term *oirad* simply denotes neighboring or adjacent populations, and *jungar* means "left wing" and refers to the left-wing position of the Oirad population. These terms are derived from the early statecraft of the nomads and highlight the territorial, rather than ethnic, foundation of the Oirad polities. In *Jangar,* the political organization is divided into left and right wings commanded by an elected supreme leader. It was not a tribal council; each key position had clearly defined administrative functions. For example, *Jangar* presents a detailed account of the office of the justiciar, which was second only to that of the khan:

> In charge of the Right Wing of the court
> Was the wise noble Golden Heart Shaman.
> Who knew the history over ninety-nine years,
> Who forecast the future for ninety-nine years to come.
> He governed the administrative jurisdictions
> Of the union's seventy khanates,
> Regulated both civil and religious affairs
> And, without Jangar's supervision,
> Resolved the most complicated judicial matters.

The justiciar performed judicial (*zarge*), civil (*tyor*), and religious (*shajin*) functions. The justiciar was a noble of great wealth and was highly educated. Unlike all other officers of the court administration, the justiciar was not one of the khan's military or household administrators (*sengche*). This was the only office whose holder was not expected to engage in military action, whereas other positions at the khan's court were required to possess both civil and military skills. The justiciar position was superior to that of any household officer except the general in charge of the left wing.

Through the use of indigenous sources such as *Jangar* and the Oirad dictionary of archaic words, we can learn about the nomadic symbols of statecraft. Archery, for instance, was an ordinary act, and over time the bow and arrow became ineffective weapons. But archery's cultural status was elevated by the use of the Hunnu-style *kibir,* or "whistling" arrow. In *Shi Ji,* Sima Qian wrote about the Hunnu leader Modun (234–174 BCE) and his innovative archery training. Modun made arrows that whistled in flight, and used them to drill his troops in shooting from horseback. The sound was created by a bulb carved from deerhorn or wood and attached to the tip. In *Jangar,* there is an intentional emphasis on the term *kibir,* "to whistle":

> Mangna Iron Head
> Released his *kibir*-whistling arrow
> From his intricately decorated blue bow,
> Made from a strong ash tree,
> As wide as a doorjamb.
> The arrow flew over the mountain pass,
> Penetrated Khongor's body,
> And reached his aorta.

The use of whistling arrows was widespread; they were known as *kabura-ya* among the samurai class in medieval Japan. In *Jangar* they are used by both the Bumba protectors and their rivals. The significance of the Hunnu aesthetic in *Jangar* suggests that the Kalmyk-Oirads recognized the Hunnu canon as their cultural capital and used the epic to preserve their nomad aesthetic over centuries, as their states fell and rose.

Jangar reveals the complex social milieu not only of a nomad, but also of a nomadic empire. In 1923, the Russian scholar Boris Vladimirtsev (1884–1931) emphasized that *Jangar* unearths from the past the apotheosis of nomadic statehood: the opulent encampments of the mighty khans, surrounded by imperial stables, administrators, traders, nobles, judges, knights, servants. *Jangar* is a poetic manifestation of the epitome of nomadic empire:

> Jangar united four governing principles.
> The statehood he created was indestructible,

> The glory of Bumba was uncontrollable,
> Spreading beyond its spacious land.

Nomadic empires are cosmopolitan in their social organization, and many of their material creations are valued precisely for their multicultural quality. In *Jangar*, after uniting seventy khanates in the Bumba union, the nomads turn to the collective project of building a palace. To build it, "the forty-two khans from the four continents brought the best six thousand and twelve masters with them." Ethical and aesthetic values are considered, as are artistic ambitions, physical capabilities, and environmental conditions. Reminding everyone about the divine forces of nature, Shaman Golden Heart intervenes in the decision making:

> It would be an empty undertaking
> To build the Khan's palace
> Reaching the sky:
> Too much is desire,
> Too far is the sky.
> The shelter for the Great Khan
> Should be three fingers below the sky!

Nomads are ever mindful of the unforgiving forces of sky, earth, and water. In the epic, the Bumba palace is built on the exact site of the "earth-water" location, on the right slope of Maikhan peak in the Tsagaan-Olom Group, on the Shar-Teg ocean shore. In order to support the height of the palace, the masters first hammer out the rock foundation and drive five foundation piles deep into the ground. The Bumba palace becomes the highest point on the world map. At the center of the palace is the *torlok,* a round tower with a domed top, which is the formal seat of the khan. *Torlok* is a specific term in Kalmyk architecture and means "soar high to the sky." The *torlok* is large enough for seven circles of six thousand and twelve heroes. Not surprisingly, its design resembles the *ger,* the nomads' tent, with sunlight and moonlight beaming through the *toono,* the crown-shaped opening at the center of the domed roof. The dome is covered in sheets of gold, so as to shine across the distance of a three-week ride.

The interior of the *torlok* is lavishly decorated. The hero's return home is often associated with the moment he enters the golden *torlok* court hall, "pushing fourteen jade-silver shutter doors, ringing five thousand door chimes."

> The boys made a gallant canter
> Around the palace.
> Pushing forteen jade-silver shutter doors,
> Ringing five thousand door chimes,
> They entered the golden *torlok* court hall.
> Great Khan Jangar greeted them warmly.

The floors are paved with coral, and the walls are covered with lion fangs, deer fangs, and pearls. The outside corners are framed with fire-red glass, the inside corners with steel. The roofs of the surrounding palace structures are covered with bright glazed tiles called *baarva*. The palace is set in the shade of a garden with five hundred sandal and poplar trees. In *Jangar* you are encouraged to find your own heroic calling and actualize that dream, including a dream of building a palace that reaches "three fingers below" the sky.

Rooted as it is in the Great Steppe Route, *Jangar* leads us into an exciting world of travels from east to west and back again. It shows not only how the steppe road was crucial to the accumulation of wealth though global trade, but also its strategic importance to the global flow of people. The quintessential elements of the Great Steppe Route were groundwater well (*ulgen*) stops, "tea and sleep" (*chai-honna*) stops, diners (*khotan*), soup kitchens (*sholun*) for monks and the poor, horse-exchange and postal stations (*yam*), watchtowers and storm shelters (*bolzatin boro*), golden and silver bridges over rivers, and jade gates marking the entrances and exits of khanates. *Jangar's* detailed accounts of nomadic palaces, cities, and empires enable readers to imagine the world of nomads free from contemporary conceptual constraints and to reconsider our understanding of nomadic polities and culture.

HERO, SPACE, TIME

In the epic tradition, a hero, or a hero-to-be, is a moving point in space. The act of becoming a hero unfolds in space, but not in time. Time in an epic is static:

> After twenty-five years of age
> The passing of time did not exist,
> The death did not enter this place.
> People did not know in Bumba
> The fierce cold of winter,

> The withering heat of summer.
> Spring followed fall.
> The wind was a reviving breeze.
> The rain was a refreshing mist.

Yet the absence of time does not limit visualization. On the contrary, being in *Jangar*'s world is epically timeless and timelessly epic. *Jangar* compensates for the missing temporal dimension with spatial imagination. The hero is a point that moves timelessly relative to the earth-water existence. Thus, *Jangar* stresses the Kalmyks' affinity with the vast open space of the Eurasian steppe.

Jangar pinpoints the Altai Mountains as the original homeland of the Oirad-Kalmyks. In the epic, the Kalmyk word for "homeland" means simply "earth-water" (*gazar-usun*). For nomads, the earth-water spatial positioning is vital. In *Jangar,* the empire is fictional, but the original home of the Kalmyk ancestors (the Oirads and the proto-Oirads) is located quite precisely:

> At the navel of the sky and the earth,
> The mountain Tsagaan Olom Maikhan,
> Shining in the sunrise,
> Rose magnificently from afar.
> The primeval ocean Shar-Teg,
> Glowing like a sacred lotus,
> Flowed its currents shallow and deep.

Today, geoscience considers the Altai glacial mountain called the Maikhan-Uul Formation of the Tsagaan-Olom Group to be the largest area of Phanerozoic (current-era) continental crustal growth in Central Asia. Thus elements of *Jangar* reveal a geographic knowledge that can be matched to today's geological maps.

As with the Maikhan peak, there is nothing mythical about the primeval Shar-Teg ocean. The Shar-Teg in southwestern Mongolia is one of the most diverse Jurassic fossil deposits in the world. Preserved in its sediment are fossils of aquatic plants, mollusks, crustaceans, insects, fishes, and amphibians. Though recent paleontological findings are inconclusive, the epic imagination tells us that this was once an ocean. As a long-lived epic, *Jangar* is deeply tectonic in its creation. It is, after all, the creation of the Altai, developed by multiple layers of terrains of different origin.

Beyond earth-water, "eternal sky" (*tengri*) is the highest force and the one that determines the order of nature and drives nomadic life and consciousness. The majestic mountains, in their proximity to the sky, emanate the divine force of nature. Nomads referred to the Tianshan range as Tengri-Khan, Sky the King. The name Tengri-Khan has disappeared from modern maps, but the great mountain knot with its ancient glacial forms is still called the Eren Habirga (Motley Ribs) Mountains. From above, the range looks like a dry carcass of ribs. The name for the Ole Mangna Tsagan Mountain has also survived. *Tsagan* means "white," and *ole* denotes a specific type of snow; the closest comparison might be the white fluffy fur of the winter hare.

Jangar traces the ancient paths of the nomads from the Indian Ocean to Mount Elbrus. The name for Elbrus, the highest mountain in Europe, is Mingi, or Thousand Mount (in Mongolic and Turkic languages), and in cycles 6 and 7, Handsome Mingian claims that he was named after Mingi. It is in the Caucasus that you can enjoy drinking the cold, fresh mountain waters of Dombay Ulgen. *Ulgen* means "a drinking stop for caravans," and a *dombay* is a long-necked drinking pitcher. In the east of the Eurasian steppe route are the Himalayas, where "in the green valleys of the mountain Samba, a herd of forty thousand dappled-gray horses, agitated, grunted and groaned as they sensed the presence of Jangar." The Rikha Samba Glacier is located in the Hidden Valley in the Mustang District of Nepal. The use of archaic words in *Jangar* highlights its transmission of geographic knowledge over time. For example, the word for "steel" in modern Kalmyk is *bold,* but in archaic Kalmyk it is *ganga.* The archaic name for the Indian Ocean is Ganga, or the Steel Silver Ocean. In *Jangar,* after passing the Himalayas, Scarlet Lion Khongor encounters the ocean:

> There was the Ganga Silver Ocean,
> Ninety-nine-spears deep at the coast.
> The Ganga Ocean's silver waves
> Flashed like the sword edges against the sun,
> The rocks giant like bulls,
> Rolled back and forth,
> And crashed, igniting the fire.

The ode to the Ganga shows how nomadic movements, whether in search of silver and steel or a love partner, are borderless in the Kalmyk collective memory and identity.

In heroic adventures, there is a constant movement. If the construct of time is missing, how does the epic conceptualize the boundaries of movement? Distance becomes a relational construct:

> Kyuder's Khanate
> Is southwest of here.
> If you send a three-year-old straw saker,
> With a thin layer of fat on her syncroup
> And three fingers of fat under her wing,
> In her journey, she would lay eggs
> And hatch chicks three times,
> But still would not reach the khanate.

Jangar presents detailed descriptions of plants, birds, and animals that are found from Siberia to the Volga River, exposing us to the nomad aesthetic that stressed unity with nature, the glory of animal freedom, and an assimilation of human nature with the nature of birds:

> The gyrfalcon placed her two black chicks
> On her *ole*-fluffy white wings.
> She sat, facing the sun,
> And kept her chicks warm.
> The gyrfalcon said:
> "In Badmin Ulan's Khanate,
> My hatchlings died three times
> Over the last three years.
> I heard that in Bumba Khanate
> The passing of time does not exist,
> Death does not enter the place.
> I will migrate to Bumba to save my chicks."

This verse reflects the spirit of the nomads, moving freely across the Eurasian steppe like migrating birds.

The rich poetic imagination of the nomads and their intimate connection with nature are also shown, for example, in the description of Jangar Khan's horse's ears: his "marvelous ears were scissor-shaped, their tips meeting in the middle," a trait of a unique breed. This breed, now almost extinct, is a fading trace of the nomadic empires. Horses with curly ears were legendary warrior steeds known for being loyal and able to find their way home, carrying an injured rider over long distances and through harsh weather.

Jangar also includes lush descriptions of trees and flowers:

> Mingian collected *za*-shrubs,
> And starting a campfire,
> Boiled a sandalwood red tea.
> Then he set up a bright-red tent.
> In its shade, stretching out like a resting belt,
> Warming up, pink like a *sukha* flower,
> He fell into a deep sleep.

Za, or saxaul, is the main arboreal cover in the Eurasian steppe and is used as firewood. *Sukha* flowers, also known as Siberian meadowsweet, grow in Eastern Siberia, the Far East, and Mongolia. Sandal and poplar trees, which are glorious in bloom, are common in the landscape of the epic. These trees are planted along the endless roads in the open steppe: "In the shade of magic sandal and poplar trees, five hundred maiden-witches approached Mingian. Offering him drinks and delights with ninety-nine hidden spells, they lured him." The trees are also planted around palaces, so heroes can dismount their horses "in the shade of sandalwood and poplar trees, grown next to the wall of the dark bronze palace." Thus, the many tales of *Jangar* unfold in the ecosystem of the Great Steppe Route.

GODS AND SLAYERS OF THE GOD OF DEATH

Given the precariousness of nomadic life, it would have been impossible for nomads not to contemplate the concepts of being and time. In *Jangar*, time is captured in relation to memorable events, such as a nostalgic identification with the primeval earth-water or a compelling call for a heroic act. The heroic act as a formal and contextual category defines all epic characters—men, women, and horses. In the absence of time, the nomadic imagination charts a conceptualization of space that evolved out of a long oral history, first following the *tengri* (sky or outer space) as the cosmic principle, and later following the Indo-Buddhist philosophical tradition known as the Nalanda school of reasoning.

Nalanda University (450–1197 CE) led the most sophisticated and important philosophical debates of the day and had an enormous influence on academic development in Inner Eurasia. The world's first residential university, it accommodated over ten thousand students and two thousand teachers and attracted international visiting scholars. In its heyday, the Great Steppe Route transmitted not only material goods but also the leading ideas of Nalanda professors.

Until very recently it was believed that Mongolic literary and Buddhist traditions originated in the thirteenth century, during the empire of Genghis Khan. However, in 2014 an international team of scholars decoded the Brahmi script of the Bugut (circa 585–587 CE) and Khuis Tolgoi (604–620 CE) rock inscriptions found in Mongolia. The language behind both Brahmi inscriptions turned out to be Mongolic. The significance of this discovery is twofold. First, it moves the time line of a Mongolic literary tradition back six hundred years. Second, it highlights the spread of Buddhist practice among the Mongolic-speaking populations, including the proto-Oirads, in the sixth century, situating them in the milieu of the Rouran (380–555 CE) and post-Rouran khanate periods.

The Oirad dictionary of archaic words and the epic of *Jangar* trace how the concept of the Buddhist meditative protector, or *yidam*, took root in the nomadic imagination. In the epic, Scarlet Lion Khongor is described as having special attributes: "the force of Mahakala was concentrated in the center of his forehead," and "the strength of Ochirvani was concentrated in the top of his head." The perfect physical training and cultural education that was passed down to heroes as "a human gift from our mothers and fathers" was not sufficient for them to be victorious. Heroes also needed to meditate to train their minds. In Sanskrit, Mahakala is the deity who overpowers the "great time-death," Yamantaka is the "slayer of the god of death," and Ochirvani is one who "holds the thunderbolt" of power. During meditation, the heroes of *Jangar* visualize *yidams*, protective deities such as Mahakala, Yamantaka, and Ochirvani, to gain the single-minded concentration needed for their heroic transformation.

Yidam is defined in the Oirad dictionary of archaic words as "sacred protector." Historically, the word carried two meanings, one physical and one transcendental. In the transcendental realm, *yidams* assume wrathful forms to vanquish Yama, the god of death. These two sides, material and transcendental, are revealed in each hero's journey. Heroes fight each other physically until they realize that the real battleground is their internal world, where the god of death must be defeated.

The Nalanda University masters Shantarakshita (725–788 CE) and Kamalasila (740–795 CE) explained in *The Stages of Meditation* how to visualize becoming Mahakala or Yamantaka, and how to cultivate the force needed to slay the god of death. In the transcendental realm of sacred protectors, everything, including selflessness and impermanence (emptiness itself), is ever changing. Meditators tune their mind to a wave of protective devotion or compassionate feeling toward others and transform that wave into impermanence. *Jangar* echoes the Nalanda masters' positive outlook and rejects the negative perspective. Heroes contemplate selflessness rather than the negation of self-existence and view impermanence as transient.

A transient nature has its order. In *Jangar*, fallen heroes, women and men, transition into other forms of being. However, they leave behind their helmets, which they liked to elegantly wear "slightly tilting to the left temple." Archaeological finds of Oirad helmets highlight the significance of the *yidam* concept of the sacred protector. The golden damascened decorations on the helmets feature Yamantaka or Mahakala in the center of the forehead. The brow of one helmet is encircled by a series of mantras, including invocations to Yamantaka. In the center of the brow is a monogram composed of ten Sanskrit syllables of the Kalachakra (wheel of time) mantra. From *Jangar*, we know how commanders wore these helmets and showed their leadership on the battleground:

> Mangna Khan sped up his horse Arak Manzin Burul
> And raced to meet Khongor.
> In front of Khongor he slowed down,
> Pulling back the silver reins in his hands,
> Gracefully turned his horse around,
> And elegantly fixed his golden helmet,
> Slightly tilting to the nape.
> The fight began.

In wearing the high-crowned helmets with the golden damascened decorations, Oirad commanders understood the power of spectacle in front of their troops that often determined the outcome of war. The *yidam* meditation helped the commanders to tune their mind to a wave of compassionate feeling toward others (their people, troops, country) and gain the single-minded concentration needed for their heroic trans-formation from mortal humans to timeless heroes on the verge of death.

THE TEN CYCLES

Prologue

The epic begins with Jangar's childhood as a captive, his consolidation of power, his marriage, and construction of the palace. After Jangar is named khan, he consolidates "the four governing principles" (*khural,* assembly or participatory government; *zargo,* the rule of law; freedom of religions and ideas; and meritocracy regardless of gender and nationality) and creates an "indestructible" statehood. Its foundation is an assembly of the scions of dynasties and heroes: Scarlet Lion Khongor, Savar Heavy Arm, Fat Belly Gyuzian Gyumbe, Serious Sanal, and Handsome Mingian.

Cycle 1: How Shaman Golden Heart
Joined Jangar's Khanate

This cycle highlights the tension and then consensus between the sacred and secular principles of governance. Shaman Golden Heart loses his theocratic power to Jangar Khan, and his role is integrated into Jangar's four governing principles. In nomadic society, sacred rep-resentatives are positioned right next to the khan; Shaman Golden Heart holds that strategic position in *Jangar.*

Cycle 2: How Scarlet Lion Khongor Got Married

This cycle, one of the longest (1,605 stanzas), is about finding true love. Love comes in all forms and shapes, and the quest for love may lead to suffering or death. Scarlet Lion Khongor becomes depressed after fail-ing to secure a marriage to the beautiful but cruel princess Zandan. The mighty warrior is transformed into a filthy boy, and his horse into a shabby colt. But both ultimately recover, and Scarlet Lion finds his karmic partner.

Cycle 3: How Scarlet Lion Khongor Fought
with Mighty Hero Jilgan Khan

Jangar seems to have complicated feelings toward Jilgan's wife, who is known not only for her humble roots, but also for the deaths of her many suitors. She warns, "Two khans, who lived in peace for seven generations, declare war for a humble woman born as a servant. Too many heroes may die. Too many horses may die." In the end, Jangar's khanate and Jilgan's khanate remain equal allied powers.

Cycle 4: How Scarlet Lion Khongor Defeated Khan Iron Head Mangna

A key part of the four governing principles was participatory governance. In this cycle, Jangar decides to admit defeat to Mangna Iron Head without any resistance. Scarlet Lion Khongor rebels against this decision: "I would rather shed my blood, which merely fills a bowl, in the last dry waterspring, than spend my life as a servant collecting fuel-dung." Sanal supports Khongor, reminding the assembly members of their oath: "We, the fiercest boars of Bumba, together tempered in the fire of wars, together shed blood of the brotherhood oath." Khongor, Sanal, Mingian, and Savar Heavy Arm overrule Jangar's decision and all of them, including Jangar, fight against Mangna Iron Head and his army.

Cycle 5: How Alya Monkhlya Stole Great Khan Jangar's Eighteen Thousand Golden Palominos

Alya Monkhlya (whose name means "rude" and "lawless bandit") comes to Bumba to steal Jangar's golden palominos, with their soft, lush manes and short-cut tails. The Bumba heroes are accustomed to wars but are not prepared for the bandit's rude language and behavior: "His vulgar shout, blaring through the air, shook the palace from the floor to the roof. It silenced the six thousand and twelve heroes, who now sat shocked in seven circles." Jangar Khan and his *bodeng* ("wild boars," an epithet commonly used to describe the heroes) win the fight against Alya Monkhlya.

Cycle 6: How Mingian, the Finest Man in the Universe, Stole Ten Thousand Pintos from Turk Khan

The Great Steppe, stretching from the Altai Mountains to the Black Sea, has witnessed some of humankind's greatest migrations and cultural transformations. Mingian represents these cultural developments. He presents himself as an immigrant who is unlike the noble *saaids* with "their familial trees ... rooted here [in Bumba] deep and tight." He laments, "I have no sister to spoil me with a delightful meal from the familial cauldron. I have no brother to miss me at home when I am away." Scarlet Lion Khongor reassures Mingian: "Are we not brothers by oath, whirling together in this life like mantras in the prayer wheel?" With the help of his oath-brothers, Mingian defeats Turk Khan and captures ten thousand pintos.

Cycle 7: How Mingian, the Finest Man in the Universe, Captured Mighty Kurmen Khan

This cycle begins as the adventure of the finest man in the universe, Mingian. The story soon shifts to the heroic adventure of Kurmen Khatun's maid, who was born and raised as a princess before Kurmen Khan subjugated her father's khanate. The maid ferociously leads a battle against Kurmen Khan and his army in Mingian's place. After their victorious return to Bumba, Mingian declines to marry the maid because she has now earned a higher social status based on her heroic deed.

Cycle 8: How Serious Sanal Defeated the Country of Half-Human Giants

Serious Sanal joins Jangar Khan's assembly, leaving his country, his high position, his father, his beautiful wife, and his daughter with cute red cheeks. In Bumba, Sanal's capabilities are indispensable: he is as wise as Shaman Golden Heart, as masterful with his axe as Savar Heavy Arm, as brave as Scarlet Lion Khongor, and as well educated and sophisticated as Handsome Mingian. Like Mingian, Sanal laments, "Before I race to the foreign land, neither a sister spoils me with a delightful meal, cooked in the ancestral cauldron, nor a brother stays behind to miss me at home," another reference to nomadic lives in migration.

Cycle 9: How Savar Heavy Arm Defeated Kilgan Khan

All *Jangar* heroes are focused and ferocious in battle, but off the battlefield, they are not afraid to show their emotions. They cry. They hug. They express their fear of being assigned to dangerous adventures. Like Khongor, Savar Heavy Arm brags when he drinks too much. Despite their individual weaknesses, each is vital to Bumba. When Jangar tactlessly elevates Khongor above the others, Savar leaves Jangar's khanate.

At the lowest point in life, heroes turn to their dear horses. Savar learns from his horse that Kilgan Khan has captured Jangar and subjugated Bumba. Savar returns to Bumba and fights Kilgan Khan.

Cycle 10: The Three Sons Captured Mighty Badmin Ulan

This cycle introduces a new generation of heroes: Scarlet Lion Khongor's son Red Khoshun; Jangar's son Black Jilgan; and Shaman Golden Heart's son Alya Shonkhor. The three battle Ulan Khan and his army. This cycle again emphasizes the importance of participatory governance and the great assembly, which recognizes the future khans based on their heroic leadership capabilities, protects the liberty of nomads, and ensures that the khan and his children are subject to common law.

FURTHER READING

The current English translation is based on the following edition with side-by-side texts in the original Kalmyk and a word-to-word translation into Russian:

Bitkeev, N., and E. Ovalov, eds. 1990. *Jangar: The Kalmyk Heroic Epic*. Moscow: The Oriental Literature Press.

Important indigenous source for archaic words in Oirad:

Muniev, B., ed. 1977. *The Kalmyk-Russian Dictionary*. Moscow: The Russian Language Press.

The original Eelian Ovla's version of *Jangar* published in Oirad script:

Ochirov, N. 1910. *Jangar by Eelian Ovla*. St. Petersburg: Saint Petersburg Press.

Poetic adaptation for a wider Russian-reading audience:

Lipkin, S. 1940. *Jangar: The Kalmyk National Epic*. Translation from Kalmyk into Russian. Moscow: Moscow Press.

Earliest published texts of *Jangar* in the West:

Bergmann, B. 1804–5. *Nomadische Streiferein unter den Kalmüken in den Jahren 1802 und 1803*. Vols. 1–2, 4:181–214. Riga.
Bobrovnikov, A. 1854. *Jangar: The Kalmyk National Tale (Vol. 5, Ch. 12)*. Translation. St. Petersburg: Bulletin of the Russian Geographic Society.

Erdmann F. 1857. "Kalmückischer Dschangar." *Zeitschrift der Deutschen morgenländischen Gesellschaft* 11 (4): 708–30.

Selected literature related to the Oirad epic:

Kichikov, A. 1992. *The Heroic Epic Jangar: A Comparative-Typological Analysis of the Monument.* Moscow: Science.

Nekljudov, S. "The Epic in World Literature." *Shagi* 1 (2): 7–22.

Vladimirtsev, B. 1923. *The Mongol-Oirad Epic.* Petrograd and Moscow: State Publishing.

Selected archaeological materials related to the Oirads:

Bobrov, L., A. Kushkumbayev, and A. Salnikov. 2018. "The Oirat Helmet of the XVII–mid-XVIII Centuries from the Akmola Regional History Museum." *Bylye Gody* 48 (2): 443–55.

Dode, Z. 2001. *The Medieval Costume of the North Caucasus People: The Historical Essays.* Moscow: Eastern Literature Publishing, Russian Academy of Science.

Gryaznov, M. 1961. "The Ancient Monuments of the Heroic Epic of the South Siberian People." *Archeological Sbornik Gosudarstvennogo Ermitazha* 3 (1): 7–31.

Kiselev, S. 1936. "Sayano-Altai Archeological Expedition." *Sovetskaya Arheologiya* 1: 282–84.

Maue, D., M. Ölmez, E. de la Vaissiere, and A. Vovin. 2017. *The Earliest Inscriptions from the Mongolian Steppe: Proceedings of the 60th Meeting of the Permanent International Altaistic Conference (PIAC), August 27–September 1, 2017, Székesfehérvár, Hungary.* Edited by Ákos Bertalan Apatóczky. Székesfehérvár, Hungary.

Selected literature related to Oirad legislation and government:

Golstunskiy, K. 1880. *The 1640 Mongol-Oirad Law.* St. Petersburg: Academy of Science Press.

Gurliand, Y. 1904. *Steppe Legislation from Ancient Times to the XVII Century.* Kazan: Kazan Press.

Krueger, J. 1972. "New Materials on the Oirat Law and History, Part One: The Jinjil Decrees." *Central Asiatic Journal* 16 (3): 194–205.

Qian, S. I. 1993. *Records of the Grand Historian.* Translated by B. Watson. New York: Columbia University Press.

Sneath, D. 2007. *The Headless State: Aristocratic Orders, Kinship Society, and the Misrepresentation of Nomadic Inner Asia.* New York: Columbia University Press.

Selected literature on Oirad culture and history:

Allsen, T. 2001. *Culture and Conquest in Mongol Eurasia.* Cambridge: Cambridge University Press.

Badmaev, A., A. Dzhalaeva, R. Dyakieva, B. Salaev, and A. Komandzhaev. 2003. *Nomto Ochirov: Life and Fate.* The Republic of Kalmykia Ministry of Education.

Boyle, J. 1958. *The History of the World Conqueror by Ata-Malik Juvaini.* Manchester: Manchester University Press.

Cleaves, F. 1982. *The Secret History of the Mongols.* Cambridge, MA. Harvard University Press.

The Dalai Lama and Kamalashila. 2019. *Stages of Meditation: The Buddhist Classic on Training the Mind.* Translated by L. Jordhen, L. Ganchenpa, and J. Russell. Boulder, CO: Shambhala Publications.

De Nicola, B. 2016. "The Queen of the Chaghatayids: Orghina Khatun and the Rule of Central Asia." *Journal of the Royal Asiatic Society* 26 (1–2): 107–20.

Korobkova, E. 2016. "Ten Great Dances of Igor Moiseyev." *Izvestiya,* January 21, 2016. https://iz.ru/news/602141.

Landa, I. 2016. "Imperial Sons-in-Law on the Move: Oyirad and Qonggirad Dispersion in Mongol Eurasia." *Archivum Eurasiae Medii Aevi* 22: 161–98.

Matuz, J. 1970. "Altan Chan und die Kalmyk in der Chronik des Seyfi Celebi." *Acta Orientalia* 32: 147–54.

Muhammad Haidar, D. 1898. *A History of the Moghuls of Central Asia.* Edited by N. Elias. Translated by E. D. Ross. London: Sampson Low, Marston.

Ponomarenko, A., D. Aristov, A. Bashkuev, et al. 2014. "Upper Jurassic Lagerstätte Shar Teg, Southwestern Mongolia." *Paleontological Journal* 48: 1573–1682.

Zlatkin, I. 1983. *The History of the Jungar Khanate, 1635–1758.* Moscow: Science Publishing.

Jangar

Jangar Khan

Prologue

It was in the beginning of times,
In the golden ancient age.
The eternity was blooming
The majestic dawns were breaking
of the holy belief of the Buddhas.

Jangar lived in these days.
He was a full orphan.
So they say about Jangar:
He was Tak-Zula Khan's descendant,
Tangsyk-Bumba Khan's grandson,
The Great Uzyunga's son.

Jangar learned early in age about war,
Whose horrors swept through his own door:
In the second summer of his life
His country fell to the cruel Monsters-Mangas.
In the third summer of his life
(His horse Aranzal turned only two),
Jangar already mounted his horse.
He rode rattling with his armor,
Destroyed three fortresses' gates,
The three-year-old orphan
Subjugated Gulidzhin-the-Monster.

In the fourth summer of his life,
Jangar crashed four fortresses' gates,
The orphan-prince
Conquered Dardingshar-the-Monster.
The fifth summer, entering the threshold,
Jangar triumphed over the five witches
and he captured the five lords.
When the prince entered
the fifth summer of his life,
Jangar was caught and held hostage by Shikshirgi.

As soon as Jangar the prince reached
The sixth summer of his life,
He demolished the six fortresses' gates,
Shattered the shafts of the forty spears.
Expanding his vast borders with force,
He conquered the Golden Tower's
Shaman Golden Heart,
And made him in charge of the Right Wing
of his countless heroic knights.
In the seventh year of his life,
He was named the great and glorious,
the Khan of the seven lands.

There were the days when his horse
Aranzal was faster than wind,
His spear was not only radiantly bright—
The radiant spear was sharply precise.
Young and famous was Jangar
Only equal to the Buddhas themselves,
Four Khans offered him
Their daughters to marry,
Nobles offered him
Their daughters to marry,
Jangar did not want to listen to them,
With nothing they withdrew away:
He married Nom Tegis's daughter—
Between the east and the south

Tegis's Khanate lay,
How to measure the expanse of his space!

About the land of Jangar they say:
There was Bumba—
Named in ancient times
Famous for horses as strong as Aranzal
Known for people as strong as giants.
The homeland of the forty khanates,
This was a sacred place.
After twenty-five years of age
The passing of time did not exist,
The death did not enter this place.
People did not know in Bumba
The fierce cold of winter,
The withering heat of summer.
Spring followed fall.
The wind was a reviving breeze.
The rain was a refreshing mist.

For happy thousand-thousands of people
the expanse of the steppe was tight
Across the five-month ride;
At the navel of the sky and the earth
The mountain Tsagaan Olom Maikhan,
Shining in the sunrise,
Rose magnificently from afar.
The primeval ocean Shar-Teg,
Glowing like a sacred lotus,
Flowed its currents shallow and deep.
There was the Cold River Dombai,
Outraging in summer,
Overflowing in winter,
To Jangar she gave her water to drink.

Jangar united four governing principles.
The statehood he created was indestructible,
The glory of Bumba was uncontrollable,

Spreading beyond its spacious land.
A mirage in the morning,
Like a golden tent,
The abode of wise Jangar
Spectacularly shone.

Once Jangar's six thousand and twelve knights discussed,
"Let's build a palace
For our lord, the Khan,
No palace in the world will be equal!"
Having assembled at the court
The khans from the forty-two khanates
Of the four continents,
All agreed to build the abode,
On the chosen spectacular site:
Along the ocean shore,
In pristine meadows,
In the shade of lush poplars,
the evergreen poplars,
Among the twelve blue seas,
To the north of the eastern rays,
At the right foot of the mountain.

The forty-two khans from the four continents
Brought the best six thousand and twelve masters with them.
First of all, the masters chose
the most holy month of the twelve months,
the most auspicious day of the thirty days,
For the future work to meet its success.
The foundation of the palace
Was paved with precious corals
To which there was no end.
The walls were erected filled with pearls.
Lions baring their fangs
were painted on the walls of the north corner.
Tigers baring their fangs
were painted on the walls of the midday corner.

Shaman Golden Heart,
Who remembers the history

Over one hundred years
Without a year that passed
Who foretells the future
For one hundred years
Without a year to come,
Respectfully intervened:
"It would be an empty undertaking
To build the Khan's palace
Reaching the sky:
Too much is desire,
Too far is the sky.
The shelter for the Great Khan
Should be three fingers below the sky!"
Six thousand and twelve masters,
Displaying the depth of the wonders,
Competing in the senses of art,
Exhausted in strength, at last,
They built the palace for Jangar.

Elevated with five towers,
Exquisitely decorated inside and outside,
Encircled with a girth like a dear horse.
The back was lined with the fire-red glass,
The façade was lined
With the cloud-white glass.
The piebald bull skin, they say,
Draped the interior of the north.
The dappled bull skin, they say,
Draped the side of the afternoon sun.

For wintering residents in the north,
Winters were easy with cow and horse milk
And on the side of the afternoon sun,
Winters were joyful with butter and fat.
Pleasing gently the senses of sight,
The fire-red glass lit
The four corners outside,
The cool-blue steel embraced
The four corners inside.

In ten colors and nine tiers,
The palace was a miracle.

But for Jangar's countless
And furious foes,
The palace was a threat.
In envy, they saw the palace
High in the sky,
Majestic like poplars,
Gleaming with gold,
And on the top
A banner floated in the wind.
When the banner was covered,
Hidden, it was radiant
Equal to one yellow sun.

When the banner was unfurled,
Released, it beamed
Equal to seven suns.
Jangar Khan resided in the palace,
Handsome as a full moon
Hero of the heroes
Harmonious among the mortals
Harsh against the foes,
Crashing them to dust.
He sat on the golden throne
And headed the court
Of the forty-four khanates.

Sovereign Khan Jangar
Striking with his looks like a moon
Silk woven robes were chosen for him
Stitched by selected highborn queens
Sewn only by his wife.
Sixteen-year-old Khatun, armed with her scissors,
Unique robes of hers made only for her loving Khan.
Khan Jangar held a general court,
Twisting the swallow-tailed ends of his mustache.
He assigned his knights

To the governing deeds,
Covering both
The mundane and sacred needs.

When Jangar's horse Aranzal
Was faster than wind,
When Jangar's spear
Was not only radiantly bright—
The radiant spear
Was sharply precise,
Young and famous Jangar
Declined forty-nine marriage offers
From the four continents
And brought Nom Tegis's daughter,
The sixteen-year-old Princess Shavdal.

Khatun (or Queen) was extraordinary:
If she looked to the left
The radiance on her left cheek
Made the little fish
Visible in the river on the left.
If she looked to the right
The radiance on her right cheek
Made the little fish
Visible in the river on the right.
Her scarlet lips
Were brighter than blood,
Her white teeth
Were whiter than snow.

The white headwear, if you believe,
Was sewn by noble queens.
The silk of her hair
Was braided to appeal your attention
To her blood-lively cheeks.
Framing elegantly on both sides
The black silk covered the braids.
The silver earrings
Swayed on her delicate earlobes

Casting the silver rays of light
On the white tenderness of her neck.
If you appreciate the cute roundness
Of the baby camel poop,
Then you may grasp the value
Of the earring design in its shape.
When Khatun,
touching the ninety-nine strings,
Began to play her silver harp,
She captivated the audience with a dream:
Flying swans above the marsh reeds
Sang and danced in circles.
You could hear in the back
Whirling geese along the lake,
Crying together before they flew
In magical twelve voices,
Enchanting with their overflowing sounds.

The *sengche* Mingian
Accompanied Khatun in her harp play.
The noble Mingian,
The son of Erke Tug,
Was the most handsome man in the Universe.
Gifted and glorious,
Superior in his talents,
He was the leading voice
Among the most famous singers.

So they said about the court.
In charge of the Right Wing of the court
Was the wise noble Golden Heart Shaman.
Who knew the history over ninety-nine years,
Who forecast the future for ninety-nine years to come.
He governed the administrative jurisdictions
Of the union's seventy khanates,
Regulated both civil and religious affairs
And, without Jangar's supervision,
Resolved the most complicated judicial matters.
Discerning the enlightenment of truth

From the darkness of lies,
Golden Heart sat on the right side
Next to the Khan.
Constantly working without a break,
He dedicated himself to Bumba,
The sacred union of the forty khanates.

Scarlet Lion Khongor
Was in charge of the Left Wing.
All enemy armies
Dispersed from Khongor in fright.
Born from Zandan Gerel (or Sandal Light),
In front of the arrows and spears,
Lion put forward
His muscular chest like a shield,
Scarlet Lion mastered his fears.
The famous giant Khongor,
Fighting alone,
Conquered seventy powers for Jangar.

Gyuzan Gyumbe, or Fat Belly,
Sat next to Scarlet Lion Khongor.
Occupying twenty seats in a confined room,
Occupying forty seats in a spacious room.
Gyuzan Fat Belly
Was known for his three assets:
His colossal power,
His coldly fierce black spear,
And his dear horse, large as an elephant,
Invisibly black in the deep night.
Gyuzan Fat Belly surprisingly won
An examination dispute
Against Golden Heart himself,
Having told the history
Of ideas and powers
Spanning the years of thousand and one.

Savar Heavy Arm
Sat to the right of Golden Heart.

A towering giant among his friends,
He was a falcon tireless in flights.
Savar Heavy Arm loved his sharp axe.
Tempered in the flames of fights,
Ready on his mighty shoulder
To swing and whack,
It was eighty and one meters in length.
Savar Heavy Arm loved his chestnut mare,
In cost it was equal
To thousand-thousands tents.
Savar threw anyone off the horse,
So great was the power of his heavy arm.

Serious Sanal,
Handsome with his dark wavy hair,
Occupied the court's third seat
On the left side,
Next to Gyuzan Fat Belly.
Serious Sanal on his dappled horse,
Followed the Conqueror of the World,
The great khan Jangar,
Leaving behind his father Bulingir.
Bulingir was deprived
Of the presence of his dear son.
Sanal's mother,
Glorious and noble,
Equal to Buddhas themselves,
Was deprived of the wake memorials
Made by her son.
In his rich country
No man could replace Noble Sanal.
His beautiful wife Angira
Was deprived of her marriage and love.

There was an assembly
Of six thousand and twelve heroes,
Scions of legendary families,
Sitting in seven circles.
There were seven circles of noble knights,

Selected from the families
Of ancient roots.
In addition, there was a circle
Of the gray-haired elderly men
And a circle
Of the red-faced honorable elderly women.
There was a circle
Of the light-faced gentle women
And finally, a circle
Of the ripe fruit-like youth.
Milk from the wild steppe mares
Formed overflowing rivers,
Strong drinks from the wild mares
Formed overflowing lakes,
Pleasing and tempting to merrymaking.
The feasts lasted long.
The drinking lasted long.
When the knights' throats,
At last, warmed up from drinking,
The multi-tiered palace
Buzzed with excitement.
The army of heroes
Began to boast of their strength,
They looked around,
Calling the neighboring circles:
"Hey, are there no battles for glory yet?
Are there no saiga-antelopes
For hunting yet?
Are there no powers left to compete?
Are there no enemies left to defeat?"

Gerel, Khongor's mother, cures wounded Jangar.

Cycle 1

How Shaman Golden Heart Joined Jangar's Khanate

There remained the only heir
From the old dynasty:
Great Prince Jangar was five years of age
When he was captured by Old Shikshirgi.
After the child was thoroughly examined
And studied from all sides
His future was revealed to Shikshirgi:
The captive was born
Among the humans to become
The only Conqueror of the World
Since the origin of the world,
Strong and famous,
The Great Khan of the seven realms.

In fear Old Shikshirgi decided to kill young Jangar.
Then five-year-old Khongor,
Old Shikshirgi's young son,
Bowed to his father's feet,
And begged to save Jangar.
Then Khongor was overjoyed to hear
That death had spared
the soul of Prince Jangar.

But Old Shikshirgi still contemplated
Ways to kill the captive,

Ways to eliminate the young prince.
Shikshirgi decided at last:
The boy will be killed
If he steals the herd of beautiful horses,
Four ten-thousands of silver-gray horses
Which belong to Golden Heart Shaman.
Inevitably, death would find the prince,
Striking him with a furious arrow,
Saturated with poison;
Shooting him with a daring arrow,
Released from the ash-tree bow.

When Prince Jangar turned six years of age,
Shikshirgi sent him on the great adventure
to hijack the four ten-thousands herd.
Jangar saddled his stallion
And sped away to the east.
Flying like a released arrow,
Aranzal threw his young rider off
The saddle, front and back.
Losing count night after night,
Losing time day after day,
Long-arched Horse Aranzal
Flew for three months without a stop.
Black dust fell behind his hooves,
Forming the horizon
That holds the Blue Sky.

After seven times seven—
Forty and nine days,
Jangar saw the mountain.
The Blue Sky leisurely rested on the top.
Climbing up the mountain,
Jangar examined with his sharp sight
Surrounding lands by four sides:
Above the mountain range,
A tower called Barvad shone from afar.

In the green valleys of the mountain Samba,

A herd of forty thousand
Dappled-gray horses
Agitated, grunted and groaned
As they sensed the presence of Jangar.
Crossing the sources of sixty river flows,
Jangar at last reached herding pastures.
Shouting, he summoned and drove the horses,
Turning them into a moving cloud.
The herd was a storm of thick dust.
As if they were envious
Of the speed of wind,
Frightened by scattered pebbles and rocks,
Anxious to touch the ashes of earth,
The wild horses galloped away.
The horses sped against the wind,
And the wind played with their manes
Like strings on a violin.
Where a skein of stallions rushed,
Sweeping red dust away with their hooves,
Paving grasslands with the crushed sand,
A trail was left behind.

Shaman Golden Heart saw this:
A horseman raced, moving a herd,
Without losing a single horse.
Ordered to saddle his horse,
Golden Heart thought:
A horseman stole my rear herd
of the dappled-gray stallions.
The rider is Prince Jangar,
Shikshirgi's captive.
Shikshirgi is behind this plan!
Seeing the future a year ahead,
Shaman thought:
If Jangar had come a year later,
Seven years of age,
He would have triumphed over me,
Held me captive,

Overthrown me in my khanate.
But he arrived here as six years old;
Hence, I will overpower him.

Shaman brought an intricately decorated weapon,
Made from the strong ash tree.
As wide as a doorjamb,
His weapon was an astonishing bow.
Golden Heart mounted his horse
With the help of his servants,
And rode his horse to the east.
After riding for forty-four days,
At last, he saw Prince Jangar
Crossing the sources of three rivers.
Immediately, Shaman released an arrow
from his bow.
The arrow flew over the river flows
Right into the boy's shoulder blade.
Loosing consciousness,
Jangar's body fell on Aranzal's soft mane.

But Aranzal saved his dear Jangar.
Exhaling mad air out of his nostrils,
The horse snorted;
Blowing the grass in front of his muzzle,
The horse raced.
Abandoning the herd of countless stallions,
Aranzal escaped with Jangar
And delivered him back
To the land of Shikshirgi.

Wounded and exhausted
Jangar fell in front of Shikshirgi.
Shikshirgi shouted furiously:
"This useless chap disgusts me.
Kill him,
Cut his bones and flesh in pieces,
Throw them to the birds and dogs!"
After ordering his wife to execute Jangar,

He put on his armor,
Mounted his dark-brown horse,
And rattling with his armor, galloped away.

When Zandan Gerel prepared to kill Jangar,
Following her husband's wish,
Her son Khongor leaped to her.
Covering Jangar's body he cried:
"Mother, kill us both!
Do not raise your hand over his body,
Extract the arrow from his shoulder blade.
You, Gerel, are a faithful wife,
Equal to Buddhas themselves,
If you, absorbed in chanting,
Step over his body three times,
The arrow will fall out of his shoulder."

Finally, Gerel conceded.
The kind mother could hear no longer
Her son's screams.
When she crossed over Jangar's body
Three times,
The arrow came out of the shoulder,
But the arrowhead stuck in the wound.
Khongor was surprised:
"Mother, the tip is still in the wound."

Zandan Gerel replied:
"Once in spring, a year after my wedding,
Something happened to me
When I went to help with the herd of mares.
I remember there was overabundance of milk.
Suddenly a strong stallion covered a mare.
Still young and reckless at that time,
Over my shoulder
I glanced at them with passion.
Perhaps, that is why the arrowhead
Stuck inside Jangar."

Folding her hands,

She became immersed in chanting
And the arrowhead fell from the wound.
Immediately Jangar was healed,
Jumping back on his strong feet
Jangar praised blessed Zandan Gerel.
Jangar and Khongor, hugging, went to feast,
Singing, they swore their blood brotherhood.

Some time passed.
Zandan Gerel was worried
That her husband had not returned.
Sadly sighing, she asked the two boys:
"Shikshirgi has not returned,
Though the time for him is to come home.
Go find him straightaway."

Jangar and Khongor
Mounted their battle horses.
Graciously rattling with their armor,
Gorgeous in their noble attire,
They galloped away.
They found Shikshirgi,
Punished by his own deeds,
Defeated by Golden Heart,
Departing with his dearest horse.
Shaman Golden Heart thought
When he saw
The two heroes-friends approaching:
If I fight with them, I will be defeated.
If Prince Jangar is united with Khongor,
My resistance will be worthless,
It is clear to me I have to give up.
Shaman untied Shikshirgi's legs,
Cantered to meet the riders.
He released the silver reins on his horses,
Then he fastened
the horses' slender forelegs
with iron hobbles out of the best iron,
And tethered them with silver fetter-locks out of the best silver.

Four great scions met
For a strategic plan.

Noble Golden Heart Shaman
Revealed his vision:
"When Great Jangar turns
Seven years of age,
No one shall compete with him.
His power will surprise us all
In this world.
Crashing countless enemies,
His name will be legendary,
His foes will be trembling,
His people will be happy.
Listen, Shikshirgi!
During this wonderful time
Engage Jangar to Princess Shavdal.
Let him take over your title,
Hand over your khanate to him,
Transfer all your governing deeds,
Both mundane and sacred needs.
When the Great Khan
Will bring all khanates for a feast,
We all will find eternal peace,
The country will happily prosper.
Jangar Khan will preside over
The governing court.
I, Golden Heart Shaman,
Will govern the court's Right Wing
Fine as a clear dream,
Scarlet Lion Khongor
Will govern the court's Left Wing.
Conquering forty powers,
We shall hold in our hands for centuries
All the works of the Universe.
Imperishable in its beauty,
Boundless in its greatness,
Bumba will shine

From generation to generation.
In the golden age of perfection,
Peaceful, content and blissful,
The glorious people of Bumba will live."

Golden Heart Shaman mounted his horse,
Rattling with his armor, he rode back home,
Driving his herd of beautiful horses,
Four ten-thousands
Of silver-gray stallions.
Jangar, Khongor, and Shikshirgi
Raced back to the Tower of Shikshirgi,
Shaped like a golden poplar tree,
the tower was prepared for a long feast.

In the seventh year of life,
Four Khans offered Jangar
Their daughters to marry,
Many nobles offered Jangar
Their daughters to marry,
Jangar did not want to listen to them,
With nothing they withdrew away:
He married Nom Tegis's daughter,
Sixteen-year-old Princess Shavdal.
Jangar Khan dedicated his life
To governing deeds,
Covering both civil and sacred needs.

In bliss and joy,
People did not know in Bumba
The fierce cold of winter,
The withering heat of summer.
The wind was a reviving breeze.
The rain was a refreshing mist.
After twenty-five years of age
The passing of time did not exist,
The death did not enter this place.

God Sky Tengri's son Togya embraces Princess Zanda in the Garuda-Eagle Tower.

How Scarlet Lion Khongor Got Married

There was an army of strong heroes,
Scions of legendary families—
Six thousand and twelve, to be precise.
There were seven circles
Of noble councilors
Selected from families of ancient roots.
In addition, there was a circle
Of the gray-haired elderly men
And a circle
Of red-faced noble elderly women,
There was a circle
Of light-faced gentle women
And finally, a circle
Of ripe fruit-like youth.
Milk from the wild steppe mares
Formed overflowing rivers,
Arza[1] from the wild mares
Formed overflowing lakes,
Pleasing and tempting to merrymaking.
The feasts were long.
The drinks lasted long.

1. A fermented milk alcoholic drink.

When the knights' throats, at last, warmed up from drinking,
The multi-tiered palace
Buzzed with excitement.
The army of heroes
Began to boast of their strength,
They looked around,
Calling to the neighboring circles:
"Hey, are there no battles for glory yet?
Are there no saiga-antelopes
For hunting yet?
Are there no powers left to compete?
Are there no enemies left to defeat?"

While heroes bragged,
Amusing themselves with questions,
And the palace buzzed with excitement,
Scarlet Lion Khongor
Declined to drink a bowl of *arza,*
Refused to utter a word of courtesy,
And sat gloomily
Until the first light of dawn.
At last, Scarlet Lion Khongor
Shared his secret thoughts with Jangar:
"Long ago I passed the threshold
Of eighteen courageous years.
There is no fire
From a single ruby-hot coal.
There is no completeness
Within a lone being.
Jangar, my dear friend,
Why am I destined
In this world to be alone?"
Smiling, Jangar Khan called:
"Where is my dear horse Aranzal?
Saddle my sorrel stallion for me!"

Famous horse-breeder Bor Mangna,
In charge of the court of the khanate stud,
Ran outside.

In the cold of spring waters,
In the velvet of grasslands,
Among the countless racehorses,
Among the dark herds,
The sorrel stallion frolicked and played.
Mangna, in charge of the horses,
Mounted the sorrel stallion,
And moving clockwise from left to right,
Made a gallant canter around the palace.
Then he fastened
The horse's slender forelegs
With iron hobbles out of the best iron,
And tethered them with silver fetter-locks out of the best silver.
He pulled the horse with forty-four men,
And brought Aranzal to the front gate.

On a saddletree panel,
Decorated with silver plaques,
Over a six-layered saddle blanket,
As spacious as a steppe,
He placed a saddle,
As large as an anvil.
Wide and comfortable,
It looked like a canyon.
The saddle was covered with a pillow
Adorned with Tibetan silver.
Along the patterned fenders,
Between the horse's prolonged ribs,
Through the eighty fine silver rings,
Bor Mangna pulled the leather straps.
When he fastened the girds so firmly,
Sweat and lather were released
From the eighty fine silver rings.
When he secured the straps so tightly,
The horse's belly
Tightened seventy-two layers of fat.
And in the end, he attached the bells
On Aranzal's mane and neck.

Aranzal's croup was divine—
The beauty of his power
Was concentrated in his croup.
Sharp precision was in his expressive eyes,
Rapid speed was in his swift feet,
His majestic sacred tail,
eighty-eight meters in length,
Rose, like a canopy, above his croup.
His slender legs were of a jerboa.
His marvelous ears were scissor-shaped,
Their tips meeting in the middle.
Aranzal played with the moon and the sun,
Catching their rays
In his thick velvet mane.
He rattled with his armor and imagined
That his four hooves tramped the enemy.
Throwing stable men to one corner,
Throwing stable men to the other corner,
The sorrel stallion
Leaped upward and forward.
Though Aranzal played,
He did not forget
About the dangerous adventure ahead of him;
Above all his assets, he was not a fool.

Shavdal Khatun,
Slender like a graceful willow,
Put her unique robe on Jangar.
Jangar praised it, admiring his wife.
The Khan grasped a whip in his grip.
When he clutched the whip so tight,
The released moisture marked the grip.
The core was plaited
With three-year-old bull leather,
The surface was made
Of four-year-old bull hide.
The texture was appealing,
Designed as patterns

On the back of a snake,
Boiled in the saliva of a snake,
Soaked in the poison of a snake—
The treated whip
Was famous for its strength.
The frame was exquisite:
There were steel buttons on it;
No one could count them at once.
A sandalwood handle had, at its end,
A wrist loop made of scarlet red silk.
A steel plate was at the end of the whip;
When it whips, it burns like fire.

Jangar said to his warriors:
"My dear Khongor desires to marry
While he is full of strength and youth.
I will go to arrange
A match with Zambal Khan
Between his daughter Zanda and Khongor."

But Golden Heart Shaman interfered:
"Do not haste, Khan.
First listen to my words.
When my horse Aksak Ulman
Was the fastest among the fast,
And I was full of youth and strength,
My khanate was not your subject
And I did not live in Jangar's Khanate.
I traveled widely
To the unknown parts of the world.
Once I reached the lands
Of three khans Sharguls
Calling the khans for a battle.
The battle did not happen then.

On my way home,
Passing the lands of Zambal Khan,
It dawned on me:
Wrestler Mongen Shikshirgi has a son, Scarlet Lion Khongor.

Only Khongor matches
To be Zambal's son-in-law.
I turned back for a moment
To glance at the child,
A three-year-old girl.
In the blink of an eye
I figured this girl out.
I did not like her at all.
In the light of fifty windows
I saw her embroidering
On the ninety-nine silks;
She was mystically
At the ninety-nine places at once.
Dead gorgeous,
Princess Zanda eclipsed an angel
With her stunning attraction.
Charming and radiant from outside,
She was filthy from inside,
Masterful in deceits,
Cursed with treacherous deeds.
Is she the only woman in the world?
Is she a real wife for Khongor?
This match will be dangerous, Khan Jangar!"

Angry, Jangar replied to Shaman:
"Against the Khan's last word
Why do you, in doubt, object?
Frightening people with prophecies,
You consider yourself a shaman.
You knew the future in the past;
You knew the past in the future;
But, I see, you have become old;
The gold of your prophecy no longer shines.
In vain your words are thrown,
Let them fly, missing all ears!"
After finishing his speech,
Jangar went out of the palace.
Forty-four horsemen

Brought Aranzal to the Khan.

Left alone, Shaman Golden Heart thought:
I see how the voyage
Will turn out to be difficult.
The battle-stallion
Will nearly starve to death.
The marrow will dry in his bones,
The fat will melt in his chest.
The great warrior
Will become exhausted from the long ride.
The steppe wind will dust his face.
The steppe heat will burn his back.
Blind and unconscious,
He will barely sit on a horseback,
Sliding from his saddle.
He will barely hold
His bright-yellow lance,
Dragging the end of the lance
On the ground.

Jangar mounted his horse,
Hardly touching the stirrup;
The toe of his blood-red
Fine-leather boot moved
As swift as a ruby coal bouncing off fire.
Aranzal flew like a blowing wind,
Slightly under the heavy clouds,
Slightly above the feather grass.
Everyone should experience
This once in life!
A leap of his hind legs
Covered the distance of one day;
A jump of his forelegs
Covered the distance of two days.
Aranzal's chest supported his chin,
When he dived,
Touching the black soil with his chin,
He snorted fire,

Burning the grass into ashes.
Then, he jumped like a white hare,
Gently brushing the young grass fields.
A stunning horse with a long-arched back was Aranzal.

Seven times seven—forty-nine days,
The sorrel stallion galloped
Without a stop.
Jangar slowed down
At the observation post—Bolzatin Boro,[2]
Stretched the silver reins
And waved with his black whip.
Flashing with his black eyes,
Jangar examined the surrounding lands
By four sides:
Between the south and the east,
Zambal Khan's Tower
Lit like a bonfire from afar.
When he focused his sight,
The silhouettes of horsemen appeared
In front of the tower,
They rushed to guard Jangar.
The Khan galloped to meet the guards.
They were one hundred
Trained and refined young men
With one hundred dromedaries,
Loaded with leather sacks of strong drinks.

Rolling out a feast carpet,
The guards invited Jangar:
"Be benevolent to us, Great Khan,
Dismount the horse,
Accept our feast,
Raise a bowl of *araka!*[3]"
Handsome like a full moon, Jangar,
Receiving their treat,

2. Public towers for observation and shelter along the steppe highway.
3. A strong alcoholic drink made from fermented milk.

Asked about their health
And cordially listened to their message:
"When our honorable Zambal Khan learned
That Jangar Khan the Great was approaching,
Zambal Khan sent us
To graciously greet you."
Jangar thanked the young men,
Bade farewell and
Headed to his destination.

At last he saw
A white temple with one thousand doors
Of the bronze palace city of Zambal Khan.
Slowing down, Aranzal,
Without bending high field grass,
Without waving low field grass,
Glided with a measured pace
And ambled with a leisured gait.

Gazing at the tower,
Jangar dismounted his horse
In the shade of three sandalwood trees
Grown against the wall of the palace.
Twenty-two responsible horsemen
Took the runner to the meadows.
Jangar, passing through the palace,
Opened twenty silver gates,
Entered the court banquet hall
And sat on the silver throne.

Two khans engaged in a conversation,
Tributes and reverences were flowing rivers
Between the two friendly lords.
In the feast of the feast,
In the bliss of joy and peace,
They drank *arza* together.
Seven merry days passed,
Seven new days shone brightly,
On the third seven days Jangar said:

"The heir of the ancient dynasty,
Zambal Khan,
In search of a camel
I ended up in your sacred khanate.
I shall not rest
Until I find the three-year-old calf.
There was a special trait—
His nostrils were pierced
When he turned three.
My loss is immeasurable.
Honor me as a brother,
Return my loss to me.
A bright-red and hot-spirited camel,
No doubt, disappeared in your khanate!"

Khan Zambal chuckled in delight,
And sensibly replied:
"If a nonexistent calf gets lost
Wandering in the steppe,
Then he becomes lazy like a cow
And will never return home.
The calf is lost in foreign meadows;
No one will find him.
It is better to ask for something else,
What can I really offer you?"
In such amusing riddles,
Seven merry days passed—
There was no end to the feast.
At the end of the celebration
Zambal Khan asked:
"Please send soon that young lad
Whom I shall call my son!"

Jangar Khan bade farewell
And headed back home.
He walked pressing the coral path
With his crimson soft leather boots.
The Earth felt heavy
From his sturdy footsteps.

The horsemen led Jangar to Aranzal
And helped him
To mount the sorrel stallion.
Jangar Khan the Great,
Holding gracefully the golden reins,
Moving respectfully clockwise
From left to right,
Made an elegant canter around the palace.
Then he galloped away,
Kicking the leather stirrups
Seven thousand times silently,
Seven thousand times loudly.
Seven days later he reached
The bright-yellow Bumba Tower.
Strong guardsmen opened
The jade-silver gate.
Beaming with the rays of moonlight,
Jangar sat on the throne.
The giant knights greeted the Khan,
Offering him *araka* to drink.
The noble and even the commoners
Waited to hear the happy news.
But the Khan did not utter a word.

For seven times seven—forty-nine days
He was immersed in his thoughts.
At last,
The Conqueror of the World announced:
"On the most auspicious day of thirty days,
Of the most holy month of twelve months,
In the most spectacular fashion and style,
Send Scarlet Lion Khongor
To Zambal's Khanate!"
In the cold of spring waters,
In the velvet of grasslands,
Khongor's horseman found
Khongor's piebald Lazy Galzan.
Lazy Galzan's croup was divine—

The beauty of his power
Was concentrated in his croup.
There was sharp precision
In his expressive eyes
And rapid speed in his swift feet.
The piebald stallion rattled his armor.
Imagining that his four hooves were
Tramping the enemy's land,
He threw stable men to one corner,
He threw stable men to the other corner,
Leaping upward and forward.

Shavdal Khatun called:
"Our groom is going to the distant land.
Let's dress him up stunningly
From head to toes!"
Scarlet Lion put on a pair
Of blood-red fine-leather boots—
No better boots
Will ever be found in the world!
One hundred ladies sewed the soles;
One thousand ladies stitched
The bootleg lining.
Had you seen the footprint
of the boots alone,
You would immediately offer
One thousand coins for them;
After seeing this masterwork on Khongor
You would give up ten thousand coins.

Over a gauzy undershirt
And three fine silk robes
He put on three layers of peacetime
And unique battle armor
Over the *ludang* silk,
He fastened the iron belt
Equal in cost to seventy horses.
He attached his sword to the belt
On his right side,

Ready to swing and strike,
It was seventy and one meters in length.
Khongor threw over his shoulders
An impeccably white cape
Valued at ten thousand yurts.
At last, he put on his golden helmet,
Slightly tilted over his left temple.

Scarlet Lion drank
From a yellow porcelain bowl,
Turning it over seventy-one times;
One and seventy men
Hardly could raise it together.
Excited, Khongor grasped
A whip in his grip.
Its core was plaited
With three-year-old bull leather;
Its surface was made
Of four-year-old bull hide.
Resembling patterns on the back of a snake,
Boiled in the saliva of a snake,
Soaked in the poison of a snake—
The treated whip
Was famous for its strength.
A steel plate was at its end;
When it whips, it burns like fire.
Its sandalwood handle had, at its end,
A wrist loop made of scarlet red silk.
Scarlet Lion Khongor
Clutched the whip so tight,
The released moisture marked the grip.

At last, the knight's throat
Warmed up from drinking.
As wide as a whip,
His veins swelled on his strong forehead.
His heated heart exhilarated,
The courage of twelve lions
Boiled inside,

Ready to break out of the cage of his chest.
His ten white fingers
Squeezed into menacing fists.
It was dangerous to touch Lion Khongor—
His fingers could tear you
Like a lion's claw!
His sharp black eyes rolled in their sockets twelve times,
Becoming precise as those
Of an attacking falcon.

The multi-tiered palace
Buzzed with excitement.
The army of brave heroes
Was in awe of the spectacle.
They examined Lion's transformation,
Guessed the colossal power of his might.
Looking around,
They called the neighboring circles:
"What are his powers?
Who is he equal in strength?"
After Scarlet Lion Khongor
Was thoroughly examined
And studied from all sides,
His qualities were revealed:
The force of Mahakala was concentrated
In the center of his forehead;
The might of Tzonkava was concentrated
In the crown of his head;
The strength of Ochirvani was concentrated
In the top of his head.
His shoulder blades were
Seventy-five meters wide;
His thighs were
Eighty-five meters wide;
His waist was
Thirty-five elbows.
The energy of twelve lions was in his body;
The power of twelve thousand witches

Was in his calves.
After Khongor was examined,
Sitting on the saddle,
Standing on the ground,
The decision was made:
There were no weaknesses.
Lion Khongor was a hero
On his horse and on his feet.
There was no equal heroic spirit
In the distant and close lands:
Lion Khongor was the pride of human heroes!
The army wished him success in his journey
And a safe return back
To the jade-silver gates of Bumba.

Scarlet Lion mounted his horse, hardly touching the stirrup:
The toe of his blood-red
Fine-leather boot moved
As swift as a ruby coal bouncing off fire.
A stunning horse was Lazy Galzan!
A leap of his hind legs
Covered the distance of one day;
A jump of his forelegs
Covered the distance of two days.
Galzan's chest supported his chin,
When he dived,
Touching the black soil with his chin,
He snorted fire,
Burning the grass into ashes.
Then, he soared like a white hare,
Gently brushing the young grass fields.

Seven times seven—forty-nine days,
The piebald galloped without a stop.
Khongor ascended the observation post
At the top of the mountain.
He dismounted,
Tying his horse to the saddlebow.
Then he fastened

The horse's slender forelegs
With iron hobbles out of the best iron,
And tethered the hind legs
With silver fetter-locks
Out of the best silver.
Khongor stretched his horse's silver reins,
Waved with his black whip.
And flashed with his black eyes.
Focusing his sight,
Lion Khongor examined
The surrounding four sides:
Between the south and the east,
Zambal Khan's Tower
Lit like a bonfire from afar.

This is Zambal's palace city.
How does Princess Zanda look like?
Khongor wondered.
Focusing his eyesight at the glass tower
Built in the shape of an eagle,
He observed a shocking scene:
God Sky Tengri's son,
Semi-God Togya
Passionately embraced Princess Zanda.
Holding a wedding ceremonial
Tibia bone in her hand,
Zanda prayed to the yellow Sun
To conceive a son from Semi-God Togya.

Looking forward to Zambal Khan's Tower
and behind to Jangar Khan's Tower,
Khongor walked anxiously back and forth.
Worried for his friend,
Lazy Galzan broke free from steel hobbles
and yawned to Khongor's ear:
"After eighteen courageous years,
You decided to become a husband.
Yet, one man's shadow
Convinced you to return home.

How would the people remember you?
Do you think that
There is no hero besides you
Who would step forward for Bumba?"

In the flame of rage,
Khongor's heart tempered into steel.
Grinding his wisdom teeth, he mounted.
Scarlet Lion roared:
"Lazy Galzan,
Bring me to Togya by tomorrow!
If you won't deliver me
By the dawn on time—
The hide from your croup
Will cover the drum;
Your eight ribs
Will become the drumsticks;
Four hooves of yours
Will be used as candleholders!"

Hearing Khongor's confident pledge,
Happy Lazy Galzan
Moved like a storm of thick dust,
Raced as if he was
Envious of the speed of wind,
Frightened by scattered pebbles and rocks,
Anxious to touch the ashes of earth.
"Okay," lazy Galzan cried.
"Until the dawn,
Manage to stay on my back.
If you, flying over my croup,
Fall on the ground,
Then blame yourself.
You shall not be my rider.
I won't regret leaving you!"
Lazy Galzan soared like an eagle,
Slightly under the heavy clouds,
Slightly above the feather grass.
Grinding the horse bit with his fangs,

Galzan flew faster than a blowing wind.
Throwing his rider off the saddle,
Front and back.
Freeing himself
From the grip of the silver reins.

By the sunset,
Khongor dismounted his horse
Next to the Glass Eagle Tower.
Then he fastened the horse's forelegs
With iron hobbles out of the best iron,
And tethered the horse's hind legs
With silver fetter-locks
Out of the best silver.
He entered the tower,
Pushing the silver shutter doors,
Ringing the door bells,
And sat on the right side.

Behind the nine sheer canopy curtains,
Under the nine silk covers on the wide bed,
Placed on the silver throne on eight legs,
In bliss and satisfaction,
Semi-god's mistress reclined.
When the door bells broke the silence,
She called:
"Who is visiting me without an invitation?
A weak stray arrow flown from afar,
With a heated red face,
With a drooling canine saliva,
With a mating spark in bull's eyes,
What a dirty dog you are, go away!"

"In search of a lost herd
I ended up in your khanate,"
Khongor replied.
"After wandering for seven times seven, forty-nine days,
I walked in the first house
To share my sad news,

Quench my thirst and give me some food."
Lying behind the nine silk covers,
God Sky Tengri's son Togya shouted:
"We have neither time nor inclination
To pour you a drink.
Fill a bowl yourself!"
Scarlet Lion drank from a porcelain bowl,
Turning it over seventy-one times,
One and seventy men
Hardly could raise it together.
The couple was impatient
Behind the nine sheer canopy curtains:
"Just drink and leave us alone at once!"
"Don't haste," said Lion Khongor.
"A guest who shares a drink
Should share a pipe!"

At last, Khongor's throat
Warmed up from drinking,
His ten white fingers
Squeezed into menacing fists.
His heated heart exhilarated,
Boling twelve courages inside,
Ready to break out of his chest cage.
Scarlet Lion Khongor called Semi-God Togya:
"You have no right to send a guest away.
I cannot see you behind the sheer curtains.
Get up! Let's play outside under the Sun!"

Raising nine curtains,
Flamboyant Semi-God Togya got up.
Carelessly dragging behind
An extravagant black fur coat,
Squinting his eye,
He approached Khongor.
Measuring the challenger with one eye,
Semi-God frowned upon him:
"Every unworthy creature
Appears here from nowhere,

Wishing the same,
At the expense of my own sins,
An equal right to fight with a semi-god!
What a nuisance!"

The son of God Sky Tengri
Slowly washed his face and hands,
Put on his battle armor,
Mounted his dear horse Asman Keeria,
And moving clockwise from left to right,
Gallantly rode to the open steppe.
When two heroes
Were crossing the wide steppe,
A melancholic thought
Caught Togya's mind:
"Death befalls a hero
In the empty solitary white space!"
Losing count night after night,
Losing time day after day,
Two knights raced without a stop.
At last, they saw Ganga Silver Ocean
And Ice White Mount.
"Those who dared argue with me
Left their bones in this mountain.
Those who dared bully me,
Colored this ocean with their blood,"
Semi-God Togya warned.

The knights began their fight.
First, the burning whips
Whistled in the air.
Immediately after,
Flashing in the light,
The yellow swords
Impaled the bodies of both knights.
Smashing downward with one powerful thrust,
From the crown to the pelvis,
The sharp blades
Sliced the knights in half.

But, as waters flow,
Uninterrupted by a slicing blade,
Drawing a sword out was just enough
For their sliced bodies to fuse at once.
Then, the golden spears pierced
the knights to the bone.
Yet, nobody won.

Furious horses crossed eight strong legs.
Furious horsemen crossed four strong arms.
Twenty fingers pierced two bodies,
Pushing and pulling,
Two heroes tried
To throw each other out of the saddle.
Yet, nobody won.
"Let's not torment our herbivorous friends.
A shoulder against shoulder,
A chest against chest,
Shall we try out hero's power,
A human gift from our mothers and fathers?"

Two knights dismounted,
Tying their horses to the saddlebows,
They changed their attire.
Togya rolled the kulan skin pants
Above his knees.
Lion Khongor rolled the deerskin pants
Above his calves.
Pulling out their intricately
Decorated blue bows,
Made from the strong ash tree,
As wide as a doorjamb,
They pointed their *kibir*-whistling arrows
Against each other.
God Sky Tengri's son said:
"Who is going to shoot first?
You, who came to challenge me,
Or I, who sat peacefully?"
"I, who came to challenge you!"

Khongor released his arrow:
It didn't pierce Togya's
Stripped muscular chest,
Bouncing away with the flattened tip.
Semi-God Togya released his arrow:
It didn't pierce Khongor's
Stripped muscular chest,
Bounced four fingers away
With the flattened tip.
Yet, nobody won.

A shoulder against shoulder,
A chest against chest,
Two heroes wrestled.
Circling like furious fighting bulls,
Grunting like ferocious fighting camels,
They threw each other over the mountain,
They threw each other over the ocean.
At last, Togya raised Khongor
Above the Earth,
Ready to crush him to the ground.
But clever Khongor
On the pinky toe of his right foot
Resisted the opponent
For four days and four nights.

Lazy Galzan
Grinded the horse bit
With his fangs,
Broke the iron hobbles
Out of the best iron,
The silver fetter-locks
Out of the best silver.
Running close to his dear friend Khongor,
He lazily yawned:
"Are you not
The grandson of Peacemaker Shirke?
Are you not
The son of Champion Wrestler Shikshirgi?

Are you not
Born from smart Zandan Khatun
At her prime twenty-two years of age?
Are you not
One who conquered seventy khanates,
Recovering your shattered bones?
Are you not
Jangar's shield and friend?
After eighteen courageous years,
You decided to become a husband,
Instead, you are a ridiculed boy.
With the fine silver halter
On the right side,
If I gallop back to Jangar Khan's palace,
They would say:
Look, the groom's horse returned
With a saddle under the horse belly.
If you give up like a stubborn coward,
What would you do with eternal shame?
How would people remember you?
Come on, Scarlet Lion,
Grab his wide tulip-red sash!
With your elbow, sharp as a bee sting,
Pierce his vertebral ridge
Around his neck!"

Scarlet Lion squeezed
His ten fingers into menacing fists.
His heated heart exhilarated,
Boiling twelve courages inside,
Ready to break out of his heart cage.
Lion Khongor grabbed
Togya's wide tulip-red sash,
And pierced with his sharp steel elbow
The enemy's vertebral ridge
Around the neck.
Pressing three more times,
The elbow tore the muscles

And reached the ridge.
But Togya touched the Earth with his toes
And jumped back on his feet.
They wrestled,
Throwing each other over shoulders.

At last, Lion Khongor
Crashed Semi-God Togya over the rock,
Leaving the body imprint on the granite.
"The last regret of a defeated man
Shall be granted."
Lion Khongor said, "Wish for mercy!"
"I wish to pull the string of your life.
I have no regrets in my life.
Now, do as you please."
Lion Khongor cut Togya's body
Into two halves,
Attached them to each side of the saddle
On Togya's horse Asman Keria,
And with two horses he sped away.

At the Glass Eagle Tower
Khongor dismounted and
Fastened both horses together.
Then he entered the tower,
Pushing the silver shutter doors,
Ringing the door bells.
Khongor hoisted the remains
On the glass doors,
Sat in front of the silver bed-throne
And took off his golden helmet.
Looking past Princess Zanda,
He timidly asked:
"After riding many days and nights,
My wavy hair is tangled.
Please, get up and comb my hair."

Princess Zanda clapping began to curse:
"Let the day come soon

When the dynasty of Shikshirgi
Disappears from the face of the Earth
Without a trace!"
She clapped once.
"You are a thief,
Who stole my destined love!
Let the day come soon,
When you, lost without knowing where to go left or right,
End your worthless life
In the Black Death Mountain!"
She clapped twice.
"You are not worth
To be shot with an arrow!
You will rot alone
In the Black Death Mountain.
Your flesh will be a prey for greedy worms.
Dry wind will scatter your ashes.
Who did send you here
To destroy all that was dear to me?
Get lost and die
In the Black Death Mountain!"
She clapped three times.
"If you wish to be
With your love forever,
Then share his destiny!"
Khongor exclaimed.
He raised his sword
And sliced the princess in half.

In silence Scarlet Lion drank
From a yellow porcelain bowl,
Turning it over seventy-one times,
One and seventy men
Hardly could raise it together.
When his throat warmed up from drinking,
Khongor lay down
On the silver bed-throne
With eight legs.

Behind the canopy silk curtains
He wept for a long time.
What shall I do?
Can I just go home?
Khongor thought.
Oh, no! My honor is lost!
I killed my bride,
Who preferred
The love of another man,
Whom I killed too.
There is no return home.
I would rather face unavoidable death
In the Black Death Mountain.
Am I even afraid of Princess Zanda's curse?
If I die from thirst, hunger,
or as a prey of beasts,
Would there not be another hero born
In the homeland of Bumba warriors?

Lion Khongor walked outside the palace,
Cut Togya's horse,
and grilled the meat on a yellow fire.
Refreshed, Khongor mounted his horse,
And slowly rode
In the dark midnight silence.
By the first ray of dawn,
He reached Zambal Khan's Tower,
Brightly lit like a bonfire.
Scarlet Lion Khongor
Twelve windows smashed with his fists,
Pulled Zambal Khan from his bed outside,
Cut three straps on his back,
Whipped the wounds three times,
And threw him back on his bed.
Lazy Galzan rode his friend to the east,
Away from this ominous place.

They were on the road
Without a stop for three months.

The piebald stallion starved to near death.
The marrow dried in his bones.
The fat melted in his chest.
Khongor grew exhausted from the long ride.
The steppe wind covered his face with dust.
The steppe heat burnt his skin on the back.
Falling from the saddle,
Blind and unconscious,
With his bright-yellow lance
Falling from his weakened hand,
Khongor slowly dragged on a horseback.
When they entered the Black Death Mountain,
Lazy Galzan collapsed on the ground,
Crushing dry roots with his chin.
Khongor fell next to his dear friend.
They stayed unconscious for four days.

Suddenly three swans
With golden heads flew above them:
"How did a human and a horse end up here?
No life exists in this desolate place!
Let's bring them back to life
With water and *arshan*,[4]
It will be a blessed deed!"
Three swans poured drinks in their mouth
And flew away to the east.
The knight and his horse
Regained consciousness.
Refreshed, Khongor mounting his horse,
Galloped away.
They were on the road
Without a stop for three months.
The piebald stallion starved to near death.
The marrow dried in his bones.
The fat melted in his chest.

4. A divine nectar drink for the gods that has purifying and healing powers for humans.

He hardly moved his legs.
Then right before them,
There was the Ganga Silver Ocean,
Ninety-nine-spears deep at the coast.
The Ganga Ocean's silver waves
Flashed like sword edges against the sun,
The rocks giant like bulls
Rolled back and forth,
And crashed, igniting the fire.

Khongor freed Lazy Galzan
In the velvet of grasslands
And in the cold of spring waters.
In the middle of the day,
Khongor took his bright-yellow lance
And walked along the coast.
When he climbed up the fringing reef,
Khongor saw Fat Whale,
Floating heavily toward the coast.
Lion Khongor ran to the water
And threw his bright-yellow lance.
The lance pierced through
The first thoracic vertebra.
Khongor raised Whale above the water.
But Fat Whale, pulling his heavy body,
Fell back to the water and swam away,
Dragging Khongor
With his lance to the deep ocean.

Hearing the splashing sounds from afar,
Lazy Galzan galloped to the ocean.
He threw his sacred majestic tail,
Eighty-eight meters in length, to Khongor,
But could not get him out
Of the deep water.
Lazy Galzan shouted:
"Pull your bright-yellow lance
Out of the fish
And save your life!"

"No, pull me out with the lance
And with the fish!"
Khongor shouted back.
A desperate horse
Drove his hind legs
Up to the groin into the ground,
And at last,
Pulled out of the ocean
The man, the lance, and the fish.
Khongor grilled the fresh meat
On a yellow fire,
Served himself and enjoyed
An extravagant dinner.
Then he set up
An impeccably white tent,
In value it was equal
To ten thousand yurts.
In its shade,
Stretching out
Like a resting belt,
Warming up pink,
Like a meadowsweet flower,
He fell into a deep sleep.

Seven times seven,
Forty-nine days,
Lazy Galzan
Tenderly woke Khongor up,
Snorting into his face.
Galzan regained his weight
In the lush pastures.
Khongor got up,
Brushed his wavy curls,
Cooked and ate the rest of the meat.
Then he mounted his horse
And rode right into the ocean.
After seven days they crossed
The Ganga Silver Ocean.

Then they were on the road
Without a stop for three months.
The piebald stallion
Starved to near death.
The marrow dried in his bones.
The fat melted in his chest.
He hardly moved his legs.

Khongor slowed down at the mountain pass,
Stretched his horse's silver reins,
Waved with his black whip.
Flashing with his black eyes.
Focusing his eyesight,
Lion Khongor examined
The surrounding four sides:
At the direction of the midday,
The Bronze Tower lit
Like a bonfire from afar.
"How is this palace
Compared with Jangar's palace?"
Khongor wondered.
The palace was five fingers wider
And one finger higher.
The Khan of this palace,
Perhaps, is the lord of one
Of the four sides of the world,
As happy as Jangar the Great.
How can I even show up in this palace?
Khongor cried with tears
As clear as *arshan*.

Khongor turned Lazy Galzan
Into a scrubby colt
And himself into a filthy boy—
Ten lice fell when he scratched
His soiled forehead,
Five lice fell when he scratched
His dirty temples.
Lazy colt *dab-dab* trotted

Toward the palace.
But could not even reach *tsakhar*,[5]
The settlement of
One hundred thousand workers
Around the bronze-silver palace-city.
Exhausted, a boy fell off his colt
In a pile of dung.

An old man from the quarter
Appeared to collect dried fuel-dung,
Sitting on the Tatar-style carriage
Drawn by a red ox.
The old man found the boy
And the colt so foul-smelling
That he turned around
And drove back home.
His old wife came outside to greet him:
"Hubby, have you forgotten
About fuel-dung?"
"There was truly a terrible stench,
Exuding from a filthy boy
And his colt in the dung pile,"
He replied.
The old woman screamed at her husband:
"So many years have passed
And you have not changed.
Why are you so naïve?
You have not fathered a child
And you refuse a son
Gifted to you by God Sky Tengri.
Bring the boy at once!"

The old woman chased him out
With a soot-black poker.
When the old man prepared
The ox carriage,
The old woman gave him

5. District for servants outside the palace city.

A leather bucket full of water:
"Offer him this to drink,
If he is thirsty."
Approaching the boy
From the wind side,
The old man called out:
"If you are alive,
Here is water for you.
I will take you to my old woman."
Collecting his last strength,
Khongor drank half of the bucket
And gave the rest to Lazy Galzan.
After the old man collected fuel-dung,
He helped the boy to mount his colt
And they slowly rode home.
Warmly greeting the child,
The old woman helped him
To get off the scrubby colt.
She carried him
Into their poor tent,
And immediately washed off
All his dirt.
In the cold of spring waters,
In the velvet of grasslands,
The old man took
The scrubby colt to stay.

Some time has passed.
Khongor saw outside
Three noble boys
Playing the *shagai*[6] game.
The Khan's and chancellors' sons
Took turns throwing
Their golden bats
Into a pile of *shagai*,
The astragalus sheep-bones.

6. Astragalus sheep bone, used for playing board and other games.

Khongor walked around the field and approached the players.
One chancellor's son said:
"Look, this scrubby boy
Dares to play the *shagai* with us."
"Well, if he wishes
To participate in a contest,
There is a custom,
We must accept him!"
Khan's son replied.

The chancellor's son invited Khongor.
"I would love to play with you!"
Khongor said.
"But do you know our rule?
For every round
We put a sack of gold.
What is your bet?
Do you still want to play?"
The chancellor's son asked.
"For one round, I will put
The ox, colt, old man,
Old woman, and myself,"
Khongor offered.
"Whether his contribution is
Small or large,
Let him play one round,"
The Khan's son decided.

Khongor received four *shagai,*
two for throwing and two for a target.
Khongor put two *shagai* on the field
And stood with other boys behind the line.
They took turns throwing the *shagai.*
First, Khongor missed the target
And lost his colt.
But when he threw again,
Squinting his left eye,
Khongor regained his colt,
Knocking out the two *shagai* at once.

After collecting his four *shagai*
From the field,
He knocked them all out again,
Winning three sacks of gold.
Khongor played two–three times more,
Losing one sack of gold at the end.
He brought the remaining
Gold back home,
One sack in his left sleeve,
One sack in his right sleeve,
And poured the gold
On his poor parents' bed.
The happy couple bought
Four kinds of livestock:
Camels, cows, horses, and sheep.
They no longer collected
The leftover food.

Once Khongor saw
Near the palace a crowd,
As dense as a thicket of reed.
The boy ran back home
And asked the old man:
"Guests overcrowded
The palace center
Like a thicket of reed,
Waiting for a royal feast.
Who is our Khan and what is his name?"
The old man replied:
"His name is Fierce White Zula,
Khan of one of the four continents.
His daughter Gerenzel
Was engaged to Wrestler Tsagan,
When she was a four-year-old.
The grandson of Mangkhan the Great,
Wrestler Tsagan
Frequently comes
With his five hundred knights,

Throws lavish feasts
In the palace city, proclaiming:
'If Princess Gerenzel agrees,
I shall marry her.
If she does not,
I shall still marry the princess!'
Yet, Princess Gerenzel
Does not confirm yes or no
To Wrestler Tsagan."
After his father's words,
The boy ran outside.
Focusing his eyesight,
Khongor saw the princess,
Sitting in the Glass Eagle Tower,
Beautiful as two suns,
Beaming with energy
Through thirty-six windows.

Later, Khongor went
To visit his dear colt
In the cold of spring waters,
In the velvet of grasslands.
On the way back home,
A fair young lady
From the Glass Eagle Tower,
Wearing an airy fine-silk cape,
Floating stunningly in the wind,
Approached the boy.
When the boy turned,
She turned following him.
When the boy walked faster,
She sped up too.
Facing the little boy,
She addressed him:
"Honorable Knight!
Wishing you an eternal peace!"
Trembling with anger,
The boy replied:

"Have you lost your mind
From your idle palace life?
Your mockery is useless here.
If you need a grown-up
For your foolish jokes,
Go and find a *tsakhar* good fellow!"
The young lady smiled:
"I recognized you,
The leading Lion among all Lions,
Scarlet Lion Khongor!
Are not you
The grandson of Peacemaker Shirke?
Are not you
The son of Champion Wrestler Shikshirgi?
Are not you
Born from smart Zandan Khatun
At her prime twenty-two years of age?
Conquering seventy khanates,
Recovering your shattered bones,
Are not you
Jangar's shield and friend?
Khan's daughter sent me
To graciously greet you.
Now, I must return."
The young lady walked back
To the palace city.
Khongor stayed behind in shock,
Listening to the disappearing sound
Of her airy fine-silk cape,
Floating stunningly in the wind.
His colt, Lazy Galzan,
Yawned and whispered:
"A lonely saiga-antelope,
that lost its herd, is fearful.
Be strong and prepare
Yourself for more encounters."
Calmed down, the boy
Had sweet dreams like a child

Sleeping between his parents.

Next day on the way back home
From the lake,
The lady from the Glass Eagle Tower,
Wearing an airy fine-silk cape,
Floating stunningly in the wind,
Again approached the boy.
Facing the little boy,
She addressed him:
"Honorable Knight!
Wishing you an eternal peace!
Khan's daughter summons you
To the Garuda Tower tonight,
When your parents fall asleep."

At night, the boy put on
His black felt coat
And went to the Garuda Tower.
Pushing the shutter doors,
He walked in the palace.
Sitting on the white silver throne,
The beautiful princess was equal
To the bright Sun,
Her pure energy blinded Khongor.
She rose from her throne,
Helping the boy to sit next to her.
Greeting hime, she asked about his health.
Then she filled a pipe,
Passed it to the guest,
And began her story:
"After eighteen courageous years,
You decided to marry Princess Zandan Gerel.
This unlucky union was not meant to be.
You were on the road
Seven times seven—forty-nine days.
When you entered the Black Death Mountain,
You stayed unconscious for many days.
Turning into a swan,

I flew to bring you back
to life with water and *arshan*.
Refreshed, you galloped again
Without a stop for three months.
Your piebald stallion
Starved to near death.
The marrow dried in his bones.
The fat melted in his chest.
Then right before you,
There was the Ganga Silver Ocean.
When you fed Lazy Galzan
In the velvet of grasslands,
I turned my wavy hair
Into the velvet of grasslands.
When you drank
In the cold of spring waters,
I turned my tears
Into the cold of spring waters.
When you caught and ate the fish,
I turned my body into the whale flesh.
I offered you my tears and my body.
You are meant to be my husband,
Not the man to whom I am engaged
Since four years of age.
After three near-death misfortunes,
You finally met me."

Khongor replied:
"If you recognized me before
As your true love,
Why have you waited so long?"
"Fine, but first you
Must be yourself!" she said.
The boy turned
Into the leading Lion
Among all Lions.
Scarlet Lion Khongor.

Sitting with poise,
He beamed with powerful energy,
Attractive as a full Moon
On the fifteenth night.
In bliss and delight
They spent their night.
At the first light of dawn,
Khongor woke up.
Turning back into a boy,
He walked back home.

Next day on the way back home
From the lake,
The lady from the Glass Eagle Tower
Again approached the boy:
"Honorable Knight!
Wishing you an eternal peace!
Khan's daughter is engaged
to Wrestler Tsagan,
Mangkhan the Great's grandson.
Wrestler Tsagan
With his five hundred knights,
Came today to throw a lavish feast
In the palace city,
To remind all about his engagement.
You are invited to the feast tonight
To sing *Jangar* about the Bumba heroes."

At night, the boy put
On his black felt coat
and went to the Eagle Tower.
The Khan's daughter and her fiancé
Personally welcomed him
In the crowded palace.
When five hundred knights
Sat on the right side
And three hundred maids
Sat on the left side,

The *jangarchi*[7] sat
In front of the Khan's throne.
After three drinks
The boy began to sing:
"It was in the beginning of times,
In the golden ancient age.
Jangar lived in these days.
There were the days when
Aranzal was faster than wind,
A spear was not only radiantly bright—
The radiant spear was sharply precise.
Among six thousand and twelve heroes,
Jangar favored the most
Scarlet Lion Khongor.
All enemy armies dispersed
From Khongor in fright.
Born from Zandan Gerel, Sandal Light,
In front of the arrows and spears,
Lion lifts forward
His muscular chest like a shield,
Scarlet Lion mastered his fears."
With these words Khongor
Could bear it no longer.
The Glass Eagle Palace
Trembled from his energized voice.
Princess Gerenzel,
Calming him down,
Nailed his coat to the ground.
Khongor got up,
Breaking the iron stakes,
And sang until the first light of dawn.
In the morning for singing *Jangar*
The boy received a thousand
Yellow-headed sheep.

Some time has passed.

7. Singer of the epic Jangar.

A pale-faced young woman
From the Glass Eagle Tower
Again approached the boy:
"Honorable Knight!
Wishing you an eternal peace!
There will be a wrestling contest tonight,
Dedicated to the royal engagement.
Princess Gerenzel asked you to fight
Against her fiancé's wrestler."
At night, the boy put on a black felt coat
and went to the Eagle Tower.
The Khan's daughter
And her fiancé came outside.
Sitting under the moonlight,
They announced:
"Wrestlers, get ready!"
Five hundred maids
Rolled down two canopy curtains.
Behind the green layers of silk,
The boy stripped his skinny body.
Behind the white layers of silk,
The giant wrestler stripped
His muscular torso.
Five hundred maids
Removed the canopy curtains.
The two athletes met at the center.
The giant wrestler cried in frustration:
"Do they want me to wrestle
Against this boy?
Am I here for an amusement
Or a real fight?"
"What is the difference,
We are equal in fight!"
Khongor replied.
The boy grabbed the giant's right arm,
Quickly turned him over the shoulder,
And threw the giant flat on the ground,
Shattering his bones.

"Who is this crook?" yelled the fiancé,
Trying to catch the boy.
But Princess Gerenzel interfered,
Taking Khongor away.
In the morning, for winning his contest,
The boy received a thousand yellow-headed sheep,
A white yurt and seven camels.
Khongor said to the old man:
"If we own two thousand sheep,
We should not live in the *tsakhar.*"
Driving a herd of two-thousand sheep,
The family migrated
To the shores of the great lake.
Khongor settled his parents
In the new white yurt
With the beautiful lake view.
Their old dilapidated tent
Was used for a dry fuel-dung storage.

In the morning,
Khongor woke up, feeling sad.
He drank tea and went to Lazy Galzan.
In front of his dear horse he sobbed,
Missing his sweet home Bumba.
Suddenly, the same lady approached the boy:
"Honorable Knight!
Wishing you an eternal peace!
Princess Gerenzel
Summons you to the palace."
At the Garuda-Eagle Tower,
Princess Gerenzel warmly received Khongor,
Offering him three cups
Of the *araka* strong drink, she said:
"Since we were four years of age,
Wrestler Mala Tsagan and I were engaged.
Waiting to marry me for so long,
Wrestler Tsagan, at last,
Received his confirmation.

What are you going to do
About it, my dear Khongor?"
The boy ran back to Lazy Galzan,
And shared his secret thoughts
With his dear friend.
"Why did I end up again in the land
With these strange customs and people?
Did not I cross the giant mountain,
Escaping from misfortunes?"
Khongor cried.

Looking far away at the mountain,
Suddenly he saw
A moving cloud of black dust.
This is a mirage:
Perhaps, my sight
Is not sharp from tears,
Khongor thought.
Wiping his eyes, he focused his sight.
Without a doubt he recognized
The particular trait
Of his friend's horse Aranzal.
Black dust fell behind his hooves,
Forming the horizon
That holds the Blue Sky.
Hugging, Khongor hid his face
In Lazy Galzan's mane:
"Should I run
To greet my dear friend Jangar?
Or should I hide
In disguise as a scrubby boy?"

Suddenly, the same lady
Approached the boy:
"Honorable Knight!
Wishing you an eternal peace!
Princess Gerenzel
Summons you to the palace."
At the Glass Eagle Tower,

Princess Gerenzel
Warmly received Khongor,
Offering him three cups
Of *araka*, she said:
"My dear Khongor,
As an honorable man,
You must be found
In a better mood."
Confused, Khongor
Returned home, saying:
"I have a fever
And need to rest."
Feeling worried and helpless,
The old man massaged
His son's feet.
The old woman massaged
Her son's head.

Jangar's voyage to find Khongor
Turned out to be difficult.
Long-arched Aranzal starved to near death.
The marrow dried in his bones.
The fat melted in his chest.
The great warrior grew
Exhausted from the long ride.
The steppe wind dusted his face.
The steppe heat burnt his back.
Falling from the saddle,
Blind and unconscious,
With his bright-yellow lance
Falling from his weakened hand,
Dragging on horseback,
Jangar reached
The bronze-silver palace gates.

Jangar the Khan announced:
"I am searching for my dear friend,
Scarlet Lion Khongor.
All enemy armies dispersed

From Khongor in fright.
Born from Zandan Gerel, Sandal Light,
In front of the arrows and spears,
Lion lifts forward
His muscular chest like a shield,
Scarlet Lion mastered his fears.
The famous hero Khongor,
Fighting alone,
Conquered seventy powers.
My dear friend Khongor left me,
Feeling indignity,
Because of mere misunderstanding
That can be easily resolved.
I traveled through khanates
Of seventy khans, whom I knew,
I traveled through khanates
Of twenty-five khans, whom I met,
Spreading my news:
If you are an ordained priest
Who knows Khongor,
You will become the abbot
Of one hundred thousand monks
In a newly built monastery
On the seaside in Bumba.
If you are a woman
Who knows Khongor,
You will live
In comfort and happiness
Equal to my Khatun Shavdal.
If you are a man
Who knows Khongor,
You will become
The Khan of one of the khanates.
Khan Fierce White Zula replied:
"No, such a hero does not live
In our khanate."
Jangar the Great cried in frustration.
Seven hundred thousand citizens

Were owed by his divine beauty:
"Who is the mother
Who gave birth to such a hero-man?
Who is the mare
That foaled such a hero-horse?"

Khongor asked the old man:
"Please, tell that stranger
On the sorrel stallion at the gate
That the hero
Whom he is looking for
Lives with us.
Bring him here at once!"
The old woman said
To her frozen husband:
"You will go,
As our child said.
Even if you die,
You won't regret
Following your woman's wish.
Hurry up, deliver the message!"
The old woman chased him out
With a soot-black poker.

The old man approached
Jangar and announced:
"The great hero
Whom you are looking for
Lives with us."
Grasping the old man
With his muzzle,
Sorrel stallion Aranzal
Pushed him to Jangar.
Jangar hugged
The old man and asked:
"Where, where should I go?"
When they arrived
At the white yurt
On the great lakeshore,

Khongor transforming
Back to himself
Greeted them outside.
Lazy Galzan,
Turning back into a hero-horse,
Snorted happily near Khongor.
Jangar and Khongor,
Embraced each other and cried,
Sharing their sad and happy news.

From thirty-two sides,
Jangar's thirty-two
Boars-heroes arrived.
The black dust fell
Behind their horses' hooves,
Covering the palace city
With a dust blanket.
In the city center Khongor's father
Wrestler Shikshirgi came,
Carrying thirty-two knights'
Armor over his shoulder.
For seven days and nights,
Reunited heroes
Shared their deep thoughts.
Jangar asked Khongor:
"Have you found a good match
For you in this khanate?"
"I have," he replied.
"Unfortunately,
She is engaged to someone else."
Thirty-two knights decided together:
"You shall marry her,
If the Khan says yes;
You shall marry her,
If the Khan says no."

Jangar the Great said:
"Handsome Mingian and I
Will visit the Khan first.

You all, bringing the feast,
Come later."
Jangar and Mingian
Mounted their stallions.
In front of
One hundred thousand *tsakhar* people,
They honorably cantered
Toward the palace.
When a young woman saw Mingian,
Blindly opening three buttons
On the side of her dress,
She followed the handsome hero.
When a mature woman saw Mingian,
Recklessly tearing three buttons
On the bosom of her dress,
She followed the handsome hero.
When an elderly woman saw Mingian,
Helplessly hitting the ground
With a leather bucket,
She followed the handsome hero,
Crying: "Oh, I am so unlucky!
If only you have crossed my path
When I was fifteen,
I would have had a chance
To make such a hero love me!"
One hundred thousand *tsakhar* people
Followed two heroes to the palace.
Jangar and Mingian,
Moving clockwise from left to right,
Made a gallant canter
Around the Abate of Buddhas.
Then they dismounted their horses
In the shade of sandalwood
And poplar trees,
Grown next to the wall
Of the dark bronze palace.
Jangar walked through the palace,
Opening fourteen silver gates,

Entered the banquet hall.
Greeting Fierce White Zula Khan,
He sat with poise,
Beautiful as the full Moon
On the fifteenth night.
Jangar's thirty-two
Boars-heroes arrived,
Bringing food and *araka*
For a lavish feast.
They sat on the right side
Of famous Mangkhan the Great,
Wrestler Tsagan's grandfather.
Jangar's diplomat Eloquent Jilgan
Sat at the door,
Neither on the right
Nor on the left side.
Jangar the Great
Asked Eloquent Jilgan:
"Don't sit at the door,
Choose a side!"
Eloquent Jilgan mediated:
If a toast maker
Sits on the right,
The ceremony will be led on behalf
Of Jangar the Great's groom.
If a toast maker
Sits on the left,
The ceremony will be led on behalf
Of Mangkhan the Great's groom.
Fierce White Zula Khan
Resolved the conflict:
"The fate of my daughter
Shall depend on the outcome
Of three rounds of contest."
Both sides agreed,
Blessing with *araka* the wedding tournament.

In the first horse-racing contest,

Sanal's horse Burul came first,
Five meters ahead of all horses.
In the second contest,
Jangar's boar-hero Mergen
Won the sharpshooting contest
With his arrows.
It was agreed that both grooms
Would wrestle in the third contest.
Jangar the Khan warned the other side:
"During the contest,
Old Wrestler Shikshirgi
Would worry for his son too much.
Have five thousand *mangas,*
Half-human giants, hold him!"
Five thousand *mangas* came.
They tied old Wrestler Shikshirgi
To the Tatar iron carriage
And held him tight.

Wrestler Tsagan and Scarlet Lion Khongor,
Stripping their muscular torsos,
Began the wrestling contest.
Groom Tsagan grasped
Khongor with all his might.
Losing, Khongor could not escape
From the tight grip.
Old Wrestler Shikshirgi,
Feeling his son's near-death pain,
Broke the iron carriage,
Pushed five thousand *mangas,*
And ran to the wrestling stage.
Old Shikshirgi grabbed Wrestler Tsagan,
Crashed his arms and legs,
And threw him on the ground.
Khongor tossed Tsagan's remnants
Into the Ganga Ocean.
There was a long heavy silence.
Mangkhan the Great turned

To Jangar the Great, saying:
"Jangar the Khan,
Today, fortune is on your side.
My only Sun set down the mountain."
Mounting his horse,
Mangkhan the Great galloped away,
Followed by his late grandson's
Five hundred knights.

On the most auspicious day of thirty days,
Of the most holy month of twelve months,
Scarlet Lion Khongor
Married Princess Gerenzel.
In the center of the palace city,
Sixty white tents
Were set for a lavish feast.
The happy wedding celebration lasted
Seven times seven—forty-nine days.
Fierce White Zula Khan asked his daughter:
"What would you like to have as your wedding gift?"
Princess Gerenzel replied:
"If you wish to give me a present,
Let me have the livestock offsprings
From the past year."
The Khan and his council
Discussed her strategic request:
"If our princess takes
The livestock offspring
To faraway lands,
Animals will follow their offspring,
Owners will follow their herds,
Nomads will migrate to Jangar's Khanate."
The council nobility accepted
Princess Gerenzel's proposal
To join Jangar's Khanate.

Jangar asked Mingian and Sanal:
"Cross a nine-months distance
To Bumba within nine days,

Deliver the great news to Bumba."
Following Mingian and Sanal,
Jangar and his thirty-two
Boars-heroes galloped away,
Covering a nine-months distance
Within nine days.
Khongor's newly wed princess,
Turning into a swan with a golden crown,
Flew after her Scarlet Lion.

Mingian and Sanal arrived
Three days earlier than planned.
On the shores of the Shirke Sea
Behind Old Shikshirgi's yurt,
They built a white tent-palace
Made of forty-four lattices
And four thousand poles,
Covered with the felt
And leopard hide.
Then Mingian and Sanal
Gathered the entire nation.
Soon Jangar and his thirty-two
Heroes arrived.
They dismounted their horses
And sat in seven circles.
Milk from the wild steppe mares
Formed overflowing rivers,
Arza-drinks from the wild mares
Formed overflowing lakes.
The feasts and drinks lasted long,
Seven times seven—forty-nine days.
At the end, Jangar,
Beautiful as a lotus,
Recited a poem of blessing
And left the celebration.

After the Khan and nobility left,
Khatun Zandan Gerel
Entertained the commoners,

Whom she hardly could fit
In the palace banquet hallways
Equal to the distance
Of a five-month ride.
At the end of the celebration,
Khatun walked the last happy guests
Out of Khongor and Gerenzel's yurt.
The Bumba people all lived happily,
The statehood they created
Was indestructible.
Bumba's glory was uncontrollable,
Rattling beyond their spacious land.

How Scarlet Lion Khongor Fought with Mighty Hero Jilgan Khan

There was an army
Of six thousand and twelve heroes,
Scions of legendary families,
Assembled in seven circles.
There were seven circles
Of noble councilors,
Selected from the families
Of ancient roots.
In addition, there was a circle
Of the gray-haired elderly men
And a circle of the red-faced
Honorable elderly women.
There was a circle
Of the light-faced gentle women
And finally, a circle
Of the ripe fruit-like youth.
Milk from the wild steppe mares
Formed overflowing rivers,
Arza from the wild mares
Formed overflowing lakes.
Pleasing and tempting to merrymaking.
The feasts were long.
The drinks lasted long.
The multi-tiered palace

Buzzed with excitement.

Scarlet Lion Khongor
Warmed up from drinking *arza* and *araka,*
Began to boast of his strength,
He looked around,
Calling the neighboring circles:
"Is there a man whom I cannot crush
With ten fingers in my fists?
Is there a man whom I can not bring
Defeated on the back of my horse?"
Jangar the Khan,
Listening to his bragging, interrupted:
"Khongor, you think that you are
The best hero among us.
If this is true,
Prove it elsewhere.
Capture mighty hero Black Jilgan Khan,
Bring him here alive!"
"I will!" replied Khongor.

In the morning,
Jangar the Khan gathered his heroes—
Six thousand and twelve noble knights
Sat in seven circles.
"Offer Khongor a drink!" ordered Jangar.
Scarlet Lion drank
From a yellow porcelain bowl,
Turning it over seventy-one times,
One and seventy men
Hardly could raise it together.

At last, the knight's throat
Warmed up from drinking,
As wide as a whip,
His veins swelled on his strong forehead,
His heated heart exhilarated,
Boiling twelve courages inside,
Ready to break out of his chest cage.

His ten white fingers
Squeezed into menacing fists.
It was dangerous to touch Lion Khongor,
Each finger could tear like a lion's claw!
His sharp black eyes rolled
In the eye sockets twelve times,
Adjusting the vision into the perception
Of an attacking falcon.
Scarlet Lion Khongor looked around,
Calling neighboring circles:
"If my dry body is lost,
Earth will benefit from a handful of ashes!
If my wounded body is lost,
Earth will benefit from a bowl of blood!
Bring me my piebald Lazy Galzan!"

A horse-breeder
From the khanate stables
Ran outside.
In the cold of spring waters,
In the velvet of grasslands,
Among the countless racehorses,
Among the dark herds,
The piebald stallion frolicked and played.
The horse-breeder mounted
The piebald stallion,
And moving clockwise from left to right,
Made a gallant canter around the palace.
Then he fastened
The horse's slender forelegs
With iron hobbles out of the best iron,
And tethered them with silver fetter-locks
Out of the best silver.
He pulled the horse with forty-four men,
And brought Lazy Galzan to the front gate.

On a saddletree panel,
Decorated with silver plaques,
Over a six-layered saddle blanket,

As spacious as a steppe,
He placed a saddle,
As large as an anvil.
Wide and comfortable,
It looked like a canyon.
The saddle was covered with a pillow
Adorned with Tibetan silver.
Along the patterned fenders,
Between the horse's prolonged ribs,
Through the eighty fine silver rings,
The horse-breeder
Pulled the leather straps.
When he fastened the girds so firmly,
Sweat and lather released
From the eighty fine silver rings.
When he secured the straps so tight,
The horse's belly tightened
Seventy-two layers of fat.
And in the end, he attached the bells
On Lazy Galzan's mane and neck.

Lazy Galzan's croup was divine—
The beauty of his power
Was concentrated in his croup.
There was sharp precision
In his expressive eyes
And rapid speed in his swift feet.
The piebald stallion rattled his armor.
Imagining that his four hooves
Were trampling the enemy's land,
He threw stable men to one corner,
He threw stable men to the other corner,
Leaping upward and forward.

Scarlet Lion put on
A pair of blood-red fine-leather boots—
No better boots
Will ever be found in the world!
One hundred ladies sewed the soles;

One thousand ladies
Stitched the bootleg lining.
Had you seen the footprint
Of the boots alone,
You would offer
One thousand coins for them;
After seeing this masterwork on Khongor
You would give ten thousand.

Over a gauzy silk undershirt
And three precious silk robes
He put on his unique battle armor.
Over a silk sash, he fastened an iron belt
Equal in cost to seventy horses.
Scarlet Lion attached
His sword to the belt;
On his right side,
Ready to swing and strike,
It was seventy and one meters in length.
Khongor threw over his shoulders
An impeccably white cape
Valued at ten thousand yurts.
At last, he put on his golden helmet,
Slightly tilted over his left temple.

Excited, Khongor grasped
A whip in his grip.
Its core was plaited
With three-year-old bull leather;
Its surface was made
Of four-year-old bull hide.
Resembling patterns on the back of a snake,
Boiled in the saliva of a snake,
Soaked in the poison of a snake—
The treated whip was famous
For its strength.
A steel plate was at its end;
When it whips, it burns like fire.
Its sandalwood handle had, at its end,

A wrist loop made of scarlet red silk.
Scarlet Lion Khongor
Clutched the whip so tight,
The released moisture marked the grip.
Jangar the Khan and his heroes
Recited a poem of blessing,
Wishing Khongor success in his journey
And safe return back
To the jade-silver gates of Bumba.

Scarlet Lion Khongor
Bade farewell and went outside.
He walked pressing the coral path
With his crimson soft leather boots.
The Earth felt heavy
From his sturdy footsteps.
The horsemen led Khongor to Lazy Galzan
And helped him
To mount the piebald stallion.

Scarlet Lion mounted his horse,
Hardly touching the stirrup;
The toe of his blood-red fine-leather boot
Moved as swift as a ruby coal
Bouncing off fire.
Holding gracefully the silver reins,
Moving clockwise from left to right
Khongor made a gallant canter
Around the palace.

Khongor galloped away,
Kicking the leather stirrups
Seven thousand times silently,
Seven thousand times shouting loudly.
A stunning horse was Lazy Galzan!
A leap of his hind legs
Covers the distance of one day;
A jump of his front legs
Covers the distance of two days.

Lazy Galzan's chest supported his chin,
When he dived,
Touching the black soil with his chin,
He snorted fire,
Burning the grass into ashes.
Then, he jumped like a white hare,
Gently brushing the young grass fields.

Seven times seven—
Forty-nine days have passed.
Khongor saw a knight
Carrying a bright-yellow banner
Followed by an army
Of one hundred men and a herd of horses.
"Who are you?" Khongor asked the knight.
"I am Khan Jilgan's horse-breeder."
After galloping for two weeks,
Khongor saw a knight
Carrying a bright-yellow banner
Followed by an army
Of one hundred men and a herd of cattle.
"Who are you?" Khongor asked the knight.
"I am Khan Jilgan's cattle-breeder."
After galloping for three weeks,
Khongor saw a knight
Carrying a bright-yellow banner
Followed by an army of one hundred men
And a herd of camels.
"Who are you?" Khongor asked the knight.
"I am Khan Jilgan's camel-breeder."

After three weeks,
Khongor saw Khan Jilgan's dog-breeder,
Carrying a bright-yellow banner
Followed by an army of one hundred men
And a pack of dogs.
After three more weeks,
Khongor saw Khan Jilgan's sheep-breeder with a flock of sheep.

Khongor galloped
To the snow-white mountaintop,
Stretched his horse's silver reins
and waved with his black whip.
Flashing with his black eyes
And sharpening his sight,
Lion Khongor examined
The surrounding four sides:
Between the south and the east,
Jilgan Khan's dome tower lit like
A bonfire from afar.
How is this palace compared with
Jangar's Bumba? wondered Khongor.
The palace was equal in structure,
But better in its exterior color and design.
Around the palace,
Eighty thousand warriors
Guarded day and night,
Stood straight like spears
Nailed to the ground.

Tears pure like *arshan*
Were falling from Khongor's eyes:
"How can I fight
Such a mighty hero Jilgan Khan?
When will I learn not to drink and brag?
If I go forward, I shall lose my life.
If I return, I shall lose my honor.
I shall fight, let the destiny decide!"
When the palace-city people fell asleep,
Khongor ran, accelerating for a kilometer,
High-jumped over the guards army,
And reached the castle eaves.
In his high jump, Khongor
Accidently touched one guard's spear.
Confused, the guard turned left and right.
But his friends-guards said:

"You are dreaming.
There is nobody here besides us."

When the internal guards
Fell asleep in the *torlok*,[1]
Penetrating through
The crevices of fourteen doors,
Khongor emerged in the *torlok* court hall.
In the dim light of the night lantern,
Thirty-five boars-heroes
Slept deeply from drinking *arza*.
Scarlet Lion drank
From a yellow porcelain bowl,
Turning it over seventy-one times,
One and seventy men
Hardly could raise it together.
At last, the knight's throat
Warmed up from drinking,
As wide as a whip,
His veins swelled on his strong forehead,
His heated heart exhilarated,
Boiling twelve courages inside,
Ready to break out of his chest cage.
His ten white fingers
Squeezed into menacing fists.
It was dangerous to touch Lion Khongor,
Each finger could tear like a lion's claw!
His sharp black eyes rolled
In the eye sockets twelve times,
Adjusting the vision into the perception
Of an attacking falcon.
Scarlet Lion Khongor recited:
"If my dry body is lost,

1. A round tower with a domed top, located at the center of the palace and serving
as a court room, with the formal seat of the Khan; a specific term in Kalmyk architecture
meaning "soar high in the sky."

Earth will benefit from a handful of ashes!
If my wounded body is lost,
Earth will benefit from a bowl of blood!"

Khongor grabbed Jilgan's Khatun,
Plunged the dagger four centimeters
Deep in her chest, saying:
"Because of you,
Jangar the Khan ignores his Khatun Shavdal.
He wants me to bring you
And kill Jilgan Khan.
Tell me at once,
Where does Jilgan hide his sword?
The sword that can kill his owner."
Khatun cried:
"This is my grave burden. Two khans,
Who lived in peace for seven generations,
Declare war for a humble woman
Born as a servant.
Too many heroes may die.
Too many horses may die."
"Show me the sword!" repeated Khongor.
"I can't do that.
Too many heroes came to fight
With him and died.
You must go back
While you are still alive,"
Khatun cried.
"I can't do that.
If I fight, I shall lose my life.
If I return, I shall lose my honor,"
Khongor said.
Khongor pulled her aorta, wrapping it around
His finger three times:
"Tell me at once!" he demanded.
Jilgan's Khatun pleaded:
"Unwrap at least once,
I cannot breathe or say a word!

I will share the secret with you,
Though I won't like to see you die.
I will share the secret with you,
Because I don't want to die.
His black sword is hidden
In the corner next to his head."

Khongor found the black sword,
Turned off the night lantern,
And cut Jilgan's right hand.
Jilgan Khan jumped on his feet
And threw Khongor to the right dungeon.
But clever Khongor
On the pinky toe of his right foot
Resisted the fall
And jumped back on his feet.
Jilgan Khan threw
Khongor to the left dungeon.
But clever Khongor
On the pinky toe of his left foot
Resisted the fall
And jumped back on his feet.
Thirty-five boars-heroes woke up.
Yawning, they decided:
"Jilgan Khan shall win
By tomorrow morning,"
and went outside to sleep.
Khongor grasped Jilgan with all his might.
Losing, Jilgan could not evade
Scarlet Lion's grip.
Khongor put Jilgan
In the yellow leather sack,
Threw it over his shoulder,
And ran over the eighty thousand spears,
Breaking the ends of spears with his feet.
Khongor reached Lazy Galzan
And attached the sack to his saddle.
As he was mounting his horse,

Many spears pierced his body.
Lazy Galzan galloped away,
Jumping in the air
Eighteen thousand times,
Landing on the ground
Eighteen thousand times.
Lazy Galzan like a loaded camel
Carried his body full of pierced spears.
When angry piebald shook his body,
The spears broke
And fell on the moving ground.
Finally, they galloped away
From the guards.

Three months have passed without a stop.
Suddenly, Jilgan Khan's boars-heroes
Caught up with Khongor.
Red Mala Hero,
Riding behind Khongor, said:
"If my battle-axe misses the target,
Let me be cursed by Jilgan's rage,
Let me be captured by the God of the Underworld!"
Red Mala, while riding, stood on stirrups
And hit Khongor's back with his axe.
Breaking seventy-two hooks of armor,
The blade hit Khongor's shoulder blade.
Honorable Khongor did not feel any pain,
When Red Mala pulled his
Axe out of his body.
Jilgan Khan's thirty-five boars-heroes
Took turns, attacking Khongor.
Khongor did not feel any pain
And galloped away.

The warrior-horse exhausted
From the long ride,
The marrow dried in his bones;
The fat melted in his chest.
Khongor turned off the road

And let his horse rest in the ash grove.
Jilgan Khan's army emerged,
Swirling like a heavy cloud,
Swarming like an ant colony.
Scarlet Lion Khongor
Was ready to fight alone.

When Lazy Galzan regained some energy,
Khongor was surrounded by seven circles
Of one hundred thousand men.
Khongor jumped on his horse
And attacked the army in the center:
Five thousand spears
Pierced Lazy Galzan's chest.
Five thousand spears
Pierced Lion Khongor's back.
Khongor, grinding his wisdom teeth,
Kicked the bright-yellow stirrups
Seven thousand times silently,
Seven thousand times screaming loudly.
Lazy Galzan from the loud sound,
Jumped in the air seven thousand times,
Landed on the ground seven thousand times.
Five thousand spears broke
And fell from Lazy Galzan's chest.
Five thousand spears broke
And fell from Lion Khongor's back.
Losing count night after night,
Losing time day after day,
Lazy Galzan flew like an arrow
Seven times seven—forty-nine days.
Crossing the Arta Zandan River,
Khongor entered his country Bumba.
At the jade-silver gate
Of the bright-yellow Bumba Tower,
Khongor dismounted his horse,
Pulled Jilgan Khan out of the yellow sack,
And nailed Jilgan's hands

And feet to the cage.
Jangar Khan sent his warriors
To guard Mighty Jilgan.
In the feast of the feast,
In the bliss of joy and peace,
Jangar and his heroes drank *arza,*
Celebrating Khongor's successful adventure.

In the middle of the night,
When guards and heroes fell asleep,
Mighty Jilgan Khan got up
And pulled the iron stakes
Out of his hands and feet.
Pushing the jade-silver gates,
He entered the Bumba palace.
Looking at the sleepy heroes, he thought:
"If I capture Scarlet Lion Khongor,
They will think that
I am angry at the true winner.
If I capture Jangar the Khan,
They will think that
I am greedy for bloody power.
If I capture Shavdal Khatun,
They will think that
I am immoral with women.
I will capture Eloquent Mediator."
Jilgan Khan tied his captive.
Throwing him over the shoulder,
He ran away,
Crossing the broad rivers with two steps,
Crossing the narrow rivers with one step.

In the morning,
Jangar and his heroes found out that
Jilgan Khan escaped with Eloquent Mediator.
Scarlet Lion Khongor called out:
"My horse Galzan is lazy,
But he always catches up with the enemies.
Bring me my warrior-horse!"

Scarlet Lion drank
From a yellow porcelain bowl,
Turning it over seventy-one times,
One and seventy men
Hardly could raise it together.
Lazy Galzan,
Enveloped in a cloud of thick dust,
As if he was envious of the speed of wind,
Frightened by scattered pebbles and rocks,
Anxious to touch the ashes of earth,
Galloped away.

Seven times seven—forty-nine days,
Khongor reached Jilgan Khan's palace.
He fastened the horse's slender forelegs
With iron hobbles out of the best iron,
Tethered them with silver fetter-locks
Out of the best silver.
Pushing loudly fourteen doors,
Khongor entered the palace.
The guards tortured Eloquent Mediator,
Trying to get any information
About Jangar Khan's army.
Khongor kicked Eloquent Mediator:
"Why did you come here without resistance?"
And sat next to Jilgan Khan.

In charge of Jilgan Khan's Right Wing
Of the court was Shaman Lotus Heart.
He was a hero,
who remembered the history over
One hundred years
Without a year that passed,
Who foretold the future for
One hundred years
Without a year to come.
Discerning the real truth
From the evil lies,
Shaman Lotus Heart said to Jilgan Khan:

"Scarlet Lion Khongor's body is
Seven times stronger,
Jilgan Khan's fate is
Seven times greater,
Your power is equal. Find peace!"
Scarlet Lion Khongor said:
"If this is true, I am for peace.
But I am not sure about you."
Jilgan Khan agreed:
"I don't want to fight. I am for peace."

Soon Jangar Khan arrived,
Carrying the yellow banner,
Followed by six thousand
And twelve noble knights.
When they all dismounted,
Jilgan Khan's forty thousand horsemen came,
Taking care of the guests' horses.
Jangar, pushing fourteen shutter doors,
Emerged in the court hall.
Greeting Jilgan Khan, he sat with poise,
Handsome like a full Moon
On the fifteenth night.
In the feast of the feast,
In the bliss of joy and peace,
They drank *arza* together.

Thirty merry days passed,
Thirty new days shone brightly.
On the third cycle of thirty days
Jilgan Khan said:
"Give Jangar Khan
And his six thousand twelve heroes
The extravagant fur coats
That cannot be found in their country!"
Two great khans declared:
"We shall help each other in wars
With powerful enemies.
We shall not interfere in wars

With weak enemies."
Jilgan Khan's six thousand heroes
Bade farewell to Jangar Khan's
Six thousand and twelve heroes.
Black dust fell behind
Their horses' hooves,
Covering the palace city
With a dust blanket.
Jangar Khan and his heroes,
Holding gracefully the golden reins,
Moved traditionally clockwise
From left to right,
Made an elegant canter around the palace.
Then they galloped away,
Kicking the bright-yellow stirrups
Seven thousand times silently,
Seven thousand times shouting loudly.
Seven times seven—
Forty-nine days later they reached
The bright-yellow Bumba Tower.
Strong guardsmen
Opened the jade-silver gate.
Beaming with the moonlight rays,
Jangar sat on the throne,
Handsome as a full Moon
On the fifteenth night.
Six thousand and twelve heroes
Assembled in seven circles.
Milk from the wild steppe mares
Formed overflowing rivers,
Arza from the wild mares
Formed overflowing lakes.
The feasts were long.
The drinks lasted long.
The multi-tiered palace
Buzzed with excitement.

How Scarlet Lion Khongor Defeated Khan Iron Head Mangna

Six thousand and twelve heroes,
Scions of legendary families,
Sat in seven circles in the court hall.
Milk from the wild steppe mares
Formed overflowing rivers,
Arza from the wild mares
Formed overflowing lakes.
When the multi-tiered palace
Buzzed with excitement,
From the northern side,
Envoy Red Sun arrived on his golden stallion.
Next to the yellow Bumba banner,
He fastened the horse's forelegs
With hobbles made of the best iron,
Tethered the horse's hind legs
With fetter-locks made of the best silver.
Pushing the jade-silver shutter doors,
Ringing five thousand door bells,
He entered the golden *torlok* court hall
And sat on the right side.
When Hero Red Sun's throat warmed up from drinking,
He got up and slowly walked back and forth.
At last, he delivered the message
On behalf of Fierce Mangna Khan,

Whose battle horse is named Roan Arak Manzin:
"Great Khan Jangar,
I heard that you have a sorrel stallion Aranzal,
I shall ride him in the remote villages.[1]
Give me Aranzal!
I heard that you have Khatun Shavdal
From the dynasty of ancient khans.
I shall have her work as my wife's maid,
Pouring water on her delicate hands.
Give me Shavdal!
I heard that you have Handsome Mingian.
His inner ocean emanates the groundswells of poise;
His inner sun emanates the magnetic attraction.
I shall have him work as a toastmaker,
Entertaining my foreign guests.
Give me Mingian!
I heard that in horse-racing contests,
Sanal's horse Burul always comes first.
I shall have the battle hero work
As a herdsman's horse in my pastures.
Give me Burul!
I heard that in *araka* celebrations,
Scarlet Lion Khongor brags of his strength.
Keeping him out of my khanate,
I shall have him work
As a mail carrier to foreign countries.
Give me Khongor!
Next year, the eighth of May is your delivery date.
If you miss the day,
My three million soldiers shall invade Bumba,
Drying Bumba Sea,
Wiping out Buddhist values.
Lost their ability to speak in disbelief,
Six thousand and twelve heroes sat silently.

Jangar the Khan, turning to the right,
Asked Golden Heart Shaman:

1. Dishonor for a warrior-horse.

"To give or not to give?"
Old Shaman replied: "Not to give?
When your father-khan was twelve
And his warrior-horse was seven,
He fought Mangna Khan,
Who was seven and his Roan Arak Manzin was three.
Your father's horse hardly escaped alive.
Your father Uzyunga Khan almost died
From three hundred wounds.
Fierce Mangna Khan,
Proved to be stronger than Uzyunga Khan.
As a champion, he victoriously cantered after the fight.
Let me remind you,
Your father threw the javelin better than you,
But he barely escaped from their fierce fight."
Scarlet Lion Khongor rose up from his seat:
"Jangar the Great,
Golden Heart Shaman's words mean 'to give.'
I would rather shed my blood,
Which merely fills a bowl,
In the last dry waterspring,
Than spend my life as a servant collecting fuel-dung."

Envoy Red Sun intruded:
"Just give me the message, I must return!"
Jangar the Khan dictated his message:
"Shavdal Khatun will be informed.
She must decide herself what is right.
Mingian with two stallions Burul and Aranzal
Will be sent to Fierce Mangna Khan.
It is impossible for us to capture Khongor.
They must come here themselves to capture Scarlet Lion."
Mounting his horse, Hero Red Sun raced back home.

Distressed, Jangar called Khongor out:
"How dare you interrupt my negotiation of peace?
My boars-heroes, capture Khongor!"
Eleven out of twelve heroes surrounded Khongor,
But Sanal protested:

"I give you no consent!
We, the fiercest boars of Bumba,
Together tempered in the fire of wars,
Together shed blood of the brotherhood oath.
When twelve of us tie him crying and harmless,
He would recite our brotherhood oath.
If I hear the sacred oath from crying Khongor,
I will throw eleven of you on the palace roof.
Don't you dare touch my brother Khongor!"
Eleven boars-heroes agreed:
"We don't want to capture Scarlet Lion,"
And left the palace.
Sanal led Khongor out of the palace city,
Bade him farewell, saying:
"You must escape before you get caught."
In the dark silence of midnight,
Scarlet Lion Khongor deserted his homeland.

Three weeks have passed.
Mingian mounted his horse Golden Sharga,
Took two battle horses Aranzal and Burul
And left Bumba palace city.
Three weeks have passed.
Mingian caught up with Khongor.
Khongor cried:
"My dear Mingian,
Let me have warrior-horse Aranzal.
One-on-one, I will fight Mangna Khan
On the White Mountain Cuddle-Erklu.
Are not we brothers by oath,
Whirling together in this life like mantras in the prayer wheel?
Riding slowly, Mingian thought for seven days:
If I give Jangar's stallion Aranzal,
I will break my brotherhood oath with Jangar.
If I keep Jangar's stallion Aranzal,
I will break my brotherhood oath with Khongor.
After following Mingian for seven days,
Khongor pulled his horse in front of Mingian,

Jumped up on Lazy Galzan,
One foot on the saddlebow, one foot on the crest.
Then he jumped on the ground, landing between two horses:
"Mingian, please, come here."
Mingian dismounted,
Tying his horse to the saddlebow.
Two oath-brothers wept, embracing each other.
Scarlet Lion Khongor, mounted Aranzal,
And galloped away, shouting from afar:
"Wait for me alive, Mingian,
On the northern side,
On the White Mountain Cuddle-Erklu!"

Khongor turned Aranzal into a shabby colt,
He turned himself into a scruffy chap.
Khongor slowed down at the mountain pass Shilte,
Stretched his horse's silver reins
and waved with his black whip.
Flashing with his black eyes and sharpening his sight,
Lion Khongor examined the surrounding four sides:
Forty-two thousand soldiers were approaching.
A red banner floated magnificently in the wind.
As Khongor was passing the army,
He overheard heroes Black Shobto and Red Sun:
"I will attack Shikshirgi,
Whose pastures are on the shores of the Shirke Sea.
You will attack Fat Belly Gumbe,
Whose pastures are on the banks of Black Cold River.
I will capture Khongor alive
And take his Gerenzel Khatun as my wife."
When Scarlet Lion Khongor heard the insult,
As wide as a whip, his veins swelled on his strong forehead,
His heated heart exhilarated,
Boiling twelve courages inside,
Ready to break out of his chest cage.
His ten white fingers squeezed into menacing fists.
His sharp black eyes rolled in the eye sockets twelve times,
Honing the vision into the precision of an attacking falcon.

Scarlet Lion threw his axe at the bannerman,
Grabbed the red banner from the fallen knight,
And galloped up to the top of White Mountain.
Black Shobto caught up with Khongor.
Riding behind him, Black Shobto stood on stirrups,
And hit Khongor's back with his axe.
Breaking seventy-two hooks of armor,
The blade hit Khongor's shoulder blade.
Hero Khongor did not feel any pain,
When Black Shobto pulled his axe out of his body.
Aranzal was faster than any horse,
Leaving far behind Shobto Khara.

Scarlet Lion Khongor found Mingian on the northern side.
Passing the red banner, he said:
"My dear Mingian, offer this banner to Jangar as my present.
I will delay the army until you return
With Jangar and his boars."
Khongor raced down the mountain to fight Black Shobto.
Khongor threw Shobto over his saddlebow,
Pushed and tied him,
And dropped him at the mountaintop.
Then, Khongor raced back to fight with envoy Red Sun.
Khongor prepared his axe,
Smashed downward with one powerful thrust,
and wounded envoy Red Sun.
Red Sun barely sat on the saddle,
Clinging to his horse's mane.
Khongor pulled his coat hem,
Threw him over his saddlebow,
And dropped the tied envoy at the mountaintop.
Over three months,
Scarlet Lion fought with forty-two heroes,
Bringing their tied bodies to the mountaintop.

At last, Mingian arrived from the northern side and
Dismounted his horse Sharga
Next to the Bumba yellow banner.
He fastened the horse's forelegs

With hobbles made of the best iron and
Tethered the horse's hind legs
With fetter-locks made of the best silver.
Pushing the jade-silver shutter doors,
Ringing five thousand door bells,
He entered the golden *torlok* court hall
And handed Jangar Khan the red banner.
Jangar Khan and his six thousand and twelve knights
Discussed for three days and nights:
"If we go against Mangna Khan's three million army,
We will die outnumbered.
If not, we will let Khongor die outnumbered."
"Let's go!" shouted Jangar.
Jangar Khan mounted Zerde, his stallion Aranzal's father,
And led his six thousand and twelve boars-heroes.
His famous horse-breeder Bor Mangna rode ahead,
Holding the Bumba yellow-golden banner.
The banner floated on the wind gloriously.
When the banner was covered,
Hidden, it was radiant equal to the yellow sun.
When the banner was unfurled,
Released, it beamed equal
to the seven suns.

When three more months passed,
Khongor decided:
"Now, I shall fight Mangna Khan!"
Scarlet Lion ferociously raced toward Mangna Khan,
Who was at the front
Of his approaching army.
Mangna Khan sped up his Arak Manzin Burul
And raced to meet Khongor.
In front of Khongor he slowed down,
Pulling back the silver reins in his hands,
Gracefully turned his horse around,
And elegantly fixed his golden helmet,
Slightly tilting to the nape.
The fight began.
Khongor, holding his axe with both hands,

Raised it above his head,
And with one powerful thrust,
Smashed Mangna's open forehead below the tilted helmet.
Mangna had an iron forehead,
Which did not bend and did not feel any pain.
Caught by surprise,
Khongor was left with firesparks from his broken blade.
Placing his axe over his shoulder,
Khongor retreated,
Galloping back to the mountaintop.

Mangna Iron Head
Released his *kibir*-whistling arrow
From his intricately decorated blue bow,
Made from a strong ash tree
As wide as a doorjamb.
The arrow flew over the mountain pass,
Penetrated Khongor's body,
And reached his aorta.
Loosing strength,
Khongor's body fell on Aranzal's soft mane.
Aranzal saved Khongor,
Bringing him to the mountaintop.
Khongor slowly dismounted,
Tied his horse to the saddlebow
And fell down on the ground.
He rested his head on the gray rock.
Bleeding, Khongor lost his consciousness.

Jangar Khan and his six thousand and twelve heroes arrived.
Savar Heavy Arm came forward.
A giant among his hero-friends,
Savar Heavy Arm loved his twelve-blades axe.
Tempered in the flames of fights,
Ready on his mighty shoulder to swing and whack,
It was eighty and one *ald*[2] in length.

---

2. A measure of length (1.5 meters) approximately equal to the span between two wide-open arms of an adult.

Savar Heavy Arm loved his chestnut mare,
In cost it was equal to thousand-thousands tents.
Savar the giant threw anyone off the horse,
So great was the power of his heavy arm.
Savar Heavy Arm, approaching Jangar, asked:
"While I am still full of youth,
And my chestnut mare Kurung Galzan is full of energy,
Allow me to fight with Mangna Khan, Jangar!"
After he asked once, twice, three times,
Jangar the Khan said: "Agreed!"

Savar Heavy Arm
Ferociously raced toward Mangna Khan,
Who was at the leading flank of his army.
Mangna Khan sped up his Arak Manzin Burul
And raced to meet Savar.
In front of Savar he slowed down,
Pulling back the golden reins in his hands,
Gracefully turned his horse around,
And elegantly fixed his golden helmet,
Slightly tilting to the nape.
The fight began.
Savar, holding his axe with both hands,
Raised it above his head,
And hit Mangna with one powerful thrust.
"Tash!" a clang hung in the air,
A fire sparked in the sky,
Twelve blades broke on Savar's axe,
Falling pathetically on the ground.
Mangna stood without a dent or pain.
Savar placed his axe over his shoulder
And retreated, galloping back to the mountaintop.

Mangna Khan chased Savar.
Riding behind Savar, Mangna stood on the stirrups
And hit Savar's back with his axe.
Breaking seventy-two hooks of armor,
The blade crushed Savar's both shoulder blades.
Kurung Galzan saved Savar,

Bringing him to the mountaintop.
Savar fell from his horse next to Khongor.
Jangar's twelve boars-heroes examined Khogor's wounds.
They fastened the twelve harness straps
To the *kibir*-whistling arrow,
Released from Mangna's intricately decorated blue bow,
Made from the strong ash tree, as wide as a doorjamb.
They pulled the arrow with the horse—
At last, the arrow came out of Khongor's body,
Khongor regained his consciousness.

Serious Sanal, handsome
With his dark wavy hair, came forward:
"Jangar the Khan,
Following you, the Conqueror of the World,
I left behind my father Bulingir,
Depriving Bulingir of the presence of his dear son.
Glorious and noble, equal to Buddhas themselves,
My mother was deprived
Of the wake memorials made by her son.
In my rich country no man could replace my noble position.
My beautiful wife Angira was deprived
Of my marriage and love.
Jangar the Khan,
Grant me consent to fulfill my dedication!
Grant me permission to fight Mangna Khan!"
Jangar the Khan said: "Agreed!"

Serious Sanal raced toward Mangna Khan
And threw his golden yellow spear at Mangna.
But fast and agile Arak Manzin Burul
Steered away from Sanal's sharp throw.
The spear missed the target, falling next to Mangna's horse.
Sanal's horse Burul Galzan
Seven times steered away from Mangna's throw.
Burul Galzan saved Sanal,
Brought him back to the mountaintop.

"Now, I shall fight Mangna Khan!" Jangar declared.

Ferociously racing toward Mangna Khan,
Jangar shouted: "Forward!"
Arak Manzin Burul was fast and agile,
Steering left and right from Jangar's sharp targeting.
But Jangar's lance was faster than the horse.
Jangar threw his bright-yellow lance.
The lance pierced through Mangna's body.
Jangar raised Mangna Khan above his horse.
His heroes shouted:
"Our Khan Jangar never lost the target from his lance!"
Mangna Khan's heroes shouted:
"Our Khan always breaks the strong lance poles!"
Inspired by his heroes,
Mangna Khan collected all his might
And pulled his strong body,
Shattering Jangar's lance into twelve sandalwood chips.

Scarlet Lion Khongor could bare it no longer.
Lion roared from the bottom of his lungs.
Khongor's roar stirred the thunderstorm in the sky,
Shook the earth from its core,
Bursted a gallbladder of the mature leopard,
Who peacefully rested in the steppe.
Scarlet Lion Khongor raced forward
And fought Mangna Khan to the end.
Jangar's twelve bravest boars
Attacked Mangna's countless army.
Jangar and his boars won the battle.
On the northern side,
On the White Mountain Cuddle-Erklu,
Mangna and his forty-two heroes accepted the oath:
"The Mangna Khanate is Bumba's subject
For one and thousand years!"
and were set free to return home.

Jangar and his boar-warriors,
Mounted their warrior-horses,
And rattling with their armor, galloped back to Bumba.
Seven days later they reached

The bright-yellow Bumba Tower.
Strong guardsmen opened the jade-silver gate.
Beaming with the rays of moonlight,
Jangar sat on the throne,
Handsome as a full Moon on the fifteenth night.
Jangar Khan's six thousand and twelve heroes
Sat in seven circles.
Milk from the wild steppe mares formed overflowing rivers,
Arza from the wild mares formed overflowing lakes.
Pleasing and tempting to merrymaking.
The feasts were long. The drinks lasted long.
When the knights' throats, at last, warmed up from drinking,
The multi-tiered palace buzzed with excitement.

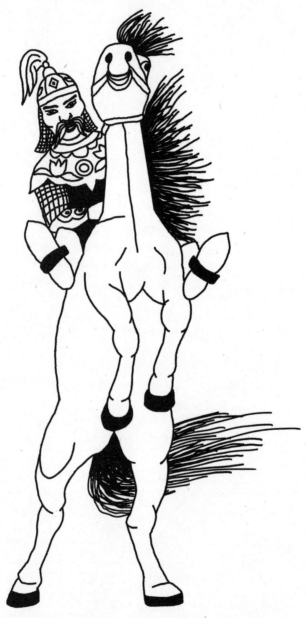

"If you, flying over my croup, fall on the ground, then blame yourself. You shall not be my rider."

Cycle 5

How Alya Monkhlya Stole Khan Jangar's Eighteen Thousand Golden Palominos

Six thousand and twelve heroes,
Scions of legendary families,
Sat in seven circles in the court hall.
Milk from the wild steppe mares
Formed overflowing rivers;
Arza from the wild mares
Formed overflowing lakes.
The multi-tiered palace
Buzzed with excitement when,
From a faraway country,
A foreigner arrived on his horse Tsiavder.
Next to the yellow Bumba banner,
He fastened the horse's forelegs
With iron hobbles out of the best iron,
Tethered the hind legs
With silver fetter-locks out of the best silver,
And entered the golden dome tower.

He pushed the jade-silver shutter doors,
Ringing five thousand door bells,
And stood in front of Jangar, shouting:
"Jangar Khan,

I am Rude Alya Monkhlya,[1]
Duutakhula's grandson,
Duuta's son.
I came here to steal
Your eighteen thousand golden palominos,
With soft lush manes and short cut tails.
If you are brave enough,
I dare you to catch me!
Otherwise, hide in Khatun Shavdal's bosom!"
Rude Alya swiftly disappeared,
His vulgar shout, blaring through the air,
Shook the palace
From the floor to the roof.

It silenced the six thousand
And twelve heroes,
Who now sat shocked in seven circles:
"Was it a devil?
Was it a joke?"
Jangar and his six thousand and twelve heroes sat silently,
Watching the herd of stallions being stolen.
"My boars: You are dear to me as life!
Let's catch the thief!" Jangar said.
But Golden Heart Shaman interfered:
"Rude Alya is Duutakhula's grandson,
Duuta's son,
And Prince Gyumbe Tsagan's leading warrior.
He has earned the Honor of Courage
Fighting wars against one hundred countries
And has earned the Honor of Hero in six countries.
If six thousand and twelve heroes
Are not prepared for a serious fight,
Rude Alya will effortlessly escape from your sight."
The khanate stable men were called to find
Six thousand and twelve hero-horses
In the cold of spring waters

---

1. Name meaning "rude" and "lawless bandit."

And in the velvet of grasslands,
Among the countless racehorses
And among the dark herds.
They brought the warrior-horses to the bright-yellow palace.
Fifty noblemen pulled Jangar's horse
With silver leads in front of all the horses.

Aranzal's croup was divine—
The beauty of his power
was concentrated in his croup.
There was sharp precision
in his expressive eyes
And rapid speed in his swift feet.
The majestic sacred tail,
eighty-eight meters in length,
Rose, like a canopy, above his croup.
His slender legs like those of a jerboa.
His marvelous ears were scissor-shaped,
Their tips meeting in the middle.

Aranzal played with the moon and the sun,
Catching their rays in his thick velvet mane.
The sorrel stallion rattled his armor.
Imagining that his four hooves
Were tramping the enemy's land,
He threw fifty *saaids*[2] to one corner,
And fifty *saaids* to the other corner,
Leaping upward and forward.
Six thousand and twelve heroes,
Gorgeous in their noble attire,
Came outside through the silver-jade gates,
They mounted their horses, hardly touching the stirrups;
The toes of their red fine-leather boots moved
As swift as ruby coals bouncing off fire.
Sitting with poise on the round saddle pillows
Adorned with Tibetan silver,
Graciously rattling with their armor,

2. Members of the nobility.

They made an honorable canter around the Buddhas,
Moving clockwise from left to right,
Recited *magtal*[3] and galloped away.
Bannerman Fierce Shankhor rode ahead,
Holding the yellow-golden Bumba banner,
Gloriously floating on the wind.
When the banner was covered,
Hidden, its radiance equaled the yellow sun.
When the banner was unfurled,
Released, it beamed equal to seven suns.

Among six thousand and twelve warrior-horses,
Savar's chestnut mare Kurung Galzan,
Sparked with uncontainable fire,
Accelerated ahead of the army.
Savar Heavy Arm, approaching Jangar, asked:
"Let me catch Rude Alya!"
Jangar the Khan said: "Agreed!"
Tash! Kurung's hooves
Covered five *beeria*[4] in one jump.
Serious Sanal, Bulingir's son,
Followed Savar on his spirited Burul.
Kurung moved like a storm of thick dust.
As if he was envious of the speed of wind,
Frightened by scattered pebbles and rocks,
Anxious to touch the ashes of earth.

At last, Savar Heavy Arm saw Rude Alya from afar,
Leading eight thousand stallions in one tight herd.
Rude Alya turned around,
Pulled his horse behind the herd,
And looked at the cloud of dust:
"This dust is from the famous mare Kurung Galzan,
Carrying Savar Heavy Arm.
Savar the giant throws anyone off the horse,
So great is the power of his heavy arm.

3. A poetry of admiration, praise, or wishing.
4. A measure of length equal to one mile.

The time has arrived to meet Jangar's tireless falcon!"

Savar Heavy Arm
Raced ferociously toward Rude Alya.
He raised his axe,
Eighty-one meters in length,
Above his head and threw it at Rude Alya.
Rude Alya's horse was faster than the axe.
The axe missed its target.
Turning around his horse,
Rude Alya released the black *kibir* arrow.
Breaking seventy-two hooks of armor,
The arrow penetrated through Savar's spinal muscles,
Almost reaching his heart.
Blood burst out of Savar's mouth.
Losing consciousness,
Savar's body fell on Kurung's soft mane.
Kurung Galzan saved Savar,
Bringing him to the mountainside.

One week passed.
Serious Sanal caught up with Rude Alya.
Riding far behind Alya, Sanal stood up on his stirrups
And threw his cold black lance at Rude Alya.
Rude Alya's horse was faster than that lance.
The lance broke, missing its target.
Rude Alya, pulling back the golden reins in his hands,
Turned his horse around.
He threw his heavy axe at Sanal,
Crashing Sanal's strong ribs and eight vertebrae bones.
Losing his Tangutan consciousness,
Sanal's body fell on Burul's soft mane.
Burul saved Sanal,
Escaping in the steppe feather reeds.

Then, Jangar and his boars arrived.
Scarlet Lion Khongor stepped forward:
"Great Khan Jangar,
You are a dream for the underworld beings,

A model for the upperworld beings,
Have I not attacked, when you said attack?
Have I not destroyed, when you said destroy?
Have I not shielded you in wars?
Allow me to fight with Rude Alya!"
"Agreed!" said Jangar Khan.
Scarlet Lion Khongor hit Alya's head with his famous whip.
Its core was plaited with three-year-old bull leather;
Its surface was made of four-year-old bull hide.
Resembling patterns on the back of a snake,
Boiled in the saliva of a snake,
Soaked in the poison of a snake—
The treated whip was famous for its strength.
Its frame was exquisite:
There were steel buttons on it;
No one could count them all at once.
Its sandalwood handle had, at its end,
A wrist loop made of scarlet red silk.
A steel plate was at its end;
When it whips, it burns like fire.
Then, pulling back the silver reins in his hands,
Turning his horse around,
Khongor hit Alya's stomach with his sword seven times.
But Rude Alya's horse was faster than the sword,
Escaping from Khongor's hits seven times.
Lion Khongor and Rude Alya
Crossed in the ferocious fight,
Circling around on their battle horses,
Cutting each other's back with heavy swords.
Their wounded bodies,
Bleeding with dark blood,
Fell on their horses' uncut mane
And rose up ready to fight again.
They fought for seven days and seven nights,
Losing bowls of red blood,
Butchering bodies into open flesh.
Yet, nobody won.

Jangar Khan could bear it no longer:
"My dear Khongor,
Are you not the grandson of Peacemaker Shirke?
Are you not the son of Champion Wrestler Shikshirgi?
Are you not born from smart Zandan Khatun
At her prime twenty-two years of age?
Conquering seventy khanates,
Recovering your shattered bones,
Are you not my shield and friend?"

Scarlet Lion Khongor cried to his horse:
"My dear Lazy Galzan,
Turn around as fast as you can!
Let me catch him rapidly, so he cannot escape!
Let me reach him with my gold-framed bright-yellow lance!
If you cannot help me,
I shall lose my Bumba home,
I shall lose my dear friend Jangar,
I shall lose my name Scarlet Lion.
Lazy Galzan raced rapidly,
Catching up closely with Rude Alya.
Khongor jumped up on Lazy Galzan,
One foot on the silver saddle pillow,
One foot on the crest.
On the tip of his golden
bright-yellow lance
He raised Rude Alya and his horse
Above his head,
And threw them to six thousand
And twelve heroes.
Then Khongor tied Alya's feet
And hands together behind the back
And attached Alya's tied body to his horse's croup.

Jangar Khan found Savar
And Sanal nearly dead
In Kundeling White Mountain Cave.
He gave Savar and Sanal the best remedy,

Called the healing *arshan* to rain,
And revived both wounded heroes.
Jangar and his boars
Mounted their warrior-horses,
And rattling with their armor,
Raced to Bumba,
Bringing back eighteen thousand
Golden palominos.
Soon they reached
The bright-yellow Bumba Tower.
Strong guardsmen opened
The jade-silver gate.
Beaming with the rays of moonlight,
Jangar sat on the throne,
Handsome as a full moon
On the fifteenth night.
Jangar Khan's six thousand
And twelve heroes sat in seven circles.
Great Jangar Khan ordered:
"Bring Rude Alya here!"
When the guards unlocked Alya's fetters,
Mighty Rude Alya
Stepped offensively on ten warriors,
Slapped boisterously five warriors,
And sat next to Shaman Golden Heart,
Who was in charge of the Right Wing.
In the feast of the feast,
They all drank *arza* together.

When the knights' throats,
At last, warmed up from drinking,
Savar Heavy Arm, a human falcon, stood up
And slapped poor Alya with the *tamga*.[5]
"Under the order of the Great Khan Jangar,
You are the subject of Bumba!
You are expected

5. A stamp that declares the subject's dependence.

To submit an annual tribute!"
Savar announced and let Rude Alya free.
The multi-tiered palace
Buzzed with excitement.
Milk from the wild steppe mares
Formed overflowing rivers
And *arza* from the wild mares
Formed overflowing lakes
Pleasing and tempting to merrymaking.
The feasting lasted long.
The drinking lasted long.

A hero drinks "from a yellow porcelain bowl, turning it over three times, seventy men hardly could raise it together."

How Mingian, the Finest Man in the Universe, Stole Ten Thousand Pintos from Turk Khan

Six thousand and twelve heroes,
Scions of legendary families,
Sat in seven circles in the court hall.
Milk from the wild steppe mares
Formed overflowing rivers,
Arza from the wild mares
Formed overflowing lakes.
When the multi-tiered palace
Buzzed with excitement,
Jangar Khan tried to hide his clear tears
Rolling down his cheeks,
Wiping them left and right
With his black silk robe sleeves.
Many nobles noticed his tears,
Pushed each other with their elbows,
Asked each other to calm down.
In charge of the Right Wing of the court,
Shaman Golden Heart turned to Khongor:
"The Lion of Lions, Scarlet Lion Khongor,
Conquering seventy khanates,
Recovering your shattered bones,
Are you not Jangar's shield and friend?
Why do you not ask the Khan
What is the reason for his tears?"

Khongor replied:
"If shaman in charge of the Right Wing of
The court would not ask
This private question,
How dare I ask the Khan?"

Eloquent Mediator Jilgan
Murmured with his plump lips:
"If you allow, I will ask the Khan."
The majority of nobles agreed: "You ask!"
Eloquent Mediator Jilgan
Three times drank from a yellow
Porcelain bowl,
Seventy men hardly could raise it together.
Three times bowed
His black head to Buddhas.
He stretched his arms wide,
Opened his dark-red palms up to the sky,
Kneeled on the silver-hemmed fluffy fur blanket and said:
"Great Khan Jangar,
Perhaps, you feel sad
Because your five-year-old Aranzal,
Foaled from the famous maiden mare,
Is not as fast as before.
Perhaps, you feel sad
Because your bright-yellow lance
Is not as sharp as before.
Perhaps, you feel sad
Because your Shavdal Khatun
Is not as gentle as before.
Perhaps, you feel sad
Because Bumba's population
In seventy khanates,
Swirling like a heavy cloud,
Swarming like an ant colony,
Is not large enough.
Perhaps, you feel sad
Because six thousand and twelve heroes

Are not as capable as before.
Perhaps, you feel sad
Because Bumba palace,
Ten tiers high and nine colors bright,
Is not marvelous enough.
Please share your private pain with us!"

Wiping his pure *arshan* tears with his
Immaculately fresh yellow scarf,
Jangar Khan opened up to numerous nobles:
"Uniting four true principles,
The statehood we created is indestructible,
The glory is uncontrollable,
Rattling beyond Bumba's spacious land.
Bumba is a miracle.
But for our countless and furious foes, Bumba is a threat.
In envy, they look at the Bumba palace
High in the sky,
Majestic like poplars
And gleaming with gold.
Three years have passed
Since Turk Altan Khan began to prepare
Ten thousand battle horses.
The pintos are rigorously
Trained for the war.
Their mouth and hooves
Do not touch the water.
In three more years
These battle horses will mature,
Turning their hooves
Into the powerful steel hooves,
Growing tails and mane
Into the flying steel wings.
Ten thousand white boars-heroes are trained
To ride the steel battle horses.
Turk Altan Khan's ten thousand pintos
Must be stolen now,
If we want to prevent our defeat

In three years!"

Shaman Golden Heart said:
"Great Khan Jangar,
You foresaw the consequences
of this military strategy.
You must choose the hero for this mission."
Jangar Khan turned to Mingian:
"My dear Mingian,
The most handsome man in the Universe,
Among six thousand and twelve strongest boars of Bumba,
Are you not one of the best heroes?
Is your horse Golden Sharga not tempered
In war flames?
Is Sharga not half a *beeria* faster
Than the speed of thought,
One *beeria* faster
Than the speed of wind?
Bring me ten thousand pintos
From Turk Altan Khan!"

Mingian sat in front with pure *arshan* tears
Rolling down his cheeks:
"Jangar, my dear Khan,
Named after Mingi Mountain,[1]
Was not I the Khan
Of the Mingi Mountain Khanate,
The Khan of ten million people,
The Khan of my own land?
After fighting with us for three weeks,
Did not you leave without a victory?
When you left with your boars,
Looking at you from the distance
Of three miles,
I saw that you were destined to become
The conqueror of all under the sun.
I relinquished my Mingi Mountain Khanate

---

1. Elbrus in the Caucasus; still called Mingi-Tau by local people.

and leadership over ten million subjects.
I left my fair-face *khatun*[2]
And my cute daughter with rosy cheeks.
Did not I follow you on my Golden Sharga,
Giving up everything that was dear to me,
Changing my khan status
To the title *sengche*?[3]
If so, why are you sending me alone
Against the colossal enemy?
Are you targeting me
Because I am rootless in Bumba?
Are you not targeting the *saaids*
Because their familial trees
Are rooted here deep and tight?
Before I race to the foreign land,
I have no sister to spoil me
With a delightful meal
From the familial cauldron,
I have no brother to miss me
At home when I am away."
Mingian sat sad with falling tears.

Savar Heavy Arm swore:
"My dear Mingian,
In this adventure,
If I stay alive, we are united as brothers!
If I die, our spirits remain united
In the better world!
Your bones shall not be lost
In the foreign land of Turk Altan.
Remember, I will wait for you on
My Kurung Galzan at the Golden Bridge!"

Scarlet Lion Khongor swore:
"My dear Mingian,
In this adventure,

---

2. Queen.
3. Chief of the household administration; in charge of ceremonies and staff.

If we are alive, we are united as brothers!
If we die, our spirits remain
United in the better world!
Your bones shall not be lost
In the foreign land of Turk Altan.
Remember, I will wait for you on
My Lazy Galzan at the Silver Bridge!"

After these encouraging words,
Mingian drank from a yellow porcelain bowl,
Turning it over three times,
Seventy men hardly could raise it together.
His heated heart exhilarated,
Boiling twelve courages inside,
Ready to break out of his chest cage.
His ten white fingers squeezed into menacing fists.
Handsome Mingian roared:
"If my dried body is lost,
Earth will benefit from a handful of ashes!
If my wounded body is lost,
Earth will benefit from a bowl of blood!
Bring me my Golden Sharga!"

A devoted horse-breeder ran outside.
In the cold of spring waters,
In the velvet of grasslands,
Among the countless racehorses,
Among the dark herds,
The palomino stallion frolicked and played.
The horse-breeder mounted Golden Sharga,
And moving clockwise from left to right,
Made an honorable canter around the palace.
Then he fastened the horse's slender
Forelegs with hobbles out of the best iron,
And tethered the hind legs
With fetter-locks made of the best silver.
He pulled the horse
With fifty *saaids'* sons,
And brought Golden Sharga

To the front gate.

On a saddletree panel,
Decorated with silver plaques,
Over a six-layered saddle blanket,
As spacious as a steppe,
He placed a saddle, as large as an anvil.
Wide and comfortable
It looked like a canyon.
The saddle was covered with a pillow
Adorned with Tibetan silver.
Along the patterned fenders,
Between the horse's prolonged ribs,
Through the eighty fine silver rings,
The horse-breeder pulled the leather straps.
When he fastened the girds so firmly,
Sweat and lather released from the eighty fine silver rings.
When he secured the straps so tight,
The horse's belly tightened seventy-two layers of fat.

Golden Palomino's croup was divine—
The beauty of his power was concentrated in his croup.
There was sharp precision in his expressive eyes
And rapid speed in his swift feet.
Golden Palomino played with the moon and the sun,
Catching their rays in his thick velvet mane.
He rattled his armor,
Imagining that his four hooves
Were tramping the enemy's land.
The palomino stallion leaped upward and forward,
Throwing *saaids*' sons to one corner,
Throwing *saaids*' sons to the other corner.

Handsome Mingian put on
A pair of blood-red fine-leather boots—
No better boots will ever be found in the world!
One hundred ladies sewed the soles;
One thousand ladies stitched the bootleg lining.
Had you seen the footprint of the boots alone,

You would offer one thousand coins for them;
After seeing this masterwork on Mingian
You would give ten thousand.
Over a festive silk undershirt and three precious robes
He put on his unique battle armor.
Over a silk sash, he fastened an iron belt
Equal in cost to seventy horses.

Mingian grasped a whip in his grip.
The core was plaited with three-year-old bull leather,
The surface was made of four-year-old bull hide.
Designed as patterns on the back of a snake,
Boiled in the saliva of a snake,
Soaked in the poison of a snake—
The treated whip was famous for its strength.
A steel plate was at the end of the whip;
When it whips, it burns like fire.
Its sandalwood handle had, at its end,
A wrist loop made of scarlet red silk.
Mingian attached his yellow sword to the iron belt.
Ready on the right side to swing and strike,
It was seventy and one *ald* in length.

Handsome Mingian, bending his knee, bowed to the throne.
Savar on the right side and Khongor on the left side,
Shoulder to shoulder, led Mingian outside the hall room.
Mingian walked pressing the coral path
With his red soft leather boots.
Pushing the jade-silver shutter doors,
Ringing the door bells, he went outside the palace.
Mingian mounted his horse, hardly touching the stirrup;
The toe of his blood-red fine-leather boot moved
As swift as a ruby coal bouncing off fire.
Six thousand and twelve heroes recited a poem of blessing,
Wishing Mingian success in his journey
And safe return back to the jade-silver gates of Bumba.

Holding gracefully the silver-bronze reins in his hands,
Moving respectfully clockwise from left to right,

Mingian made an honorable canter around the palace,
And rode to the monastery with one hundred thousand monks
on the shores of the Bumba Sea.
Next to Lama Yellow Talba's residence
He dismounted, tying his horse to the saddlebow.
Mingian walked around the temple three times,
Bowed to Buddhas three times,
Left one bar of gold on the altar,
Drank *arshan* from the pitcher to gain ninety-nine strengths,
And said to the abbot of the monastery:
"I am going alone against the colossal foreign enemy.
My Mingi Mountain and one hundred thousand workers
Shall remain with your monastery.
Please recite three times a month for me
The Eight Fierce Protectors Mantra."
The abbot blessed Mingian,
Wishing Mingian success in his journey
And safe return back to the jade-silver gates of Bumba.
Handsome Mingian, mounting his horse,
Galloped away toward the northwest.

Golden Sharga flew like a blowing wind,
Slightly under the heavy clouds,
Slightly above the feather grass.
A leap of his hind legs covers the distance of one day;
A jump of his front legs covers the distance of two days.
Golden Sharga's chest supported his chin,
When he dived, touching the black soil with his chin,
He snorted fire, burning the grass into ashes.
Then, he jumped like a white hare,
Gently brushing the young grass fields.
The stallion galloped without a stop for three weeks.

At the observation post Bolzatin Boro, Mingian dismounted,
Tying his horse to the saddlebow.
Then he fastened the horse's slender front legs
With iron hobbles out of the best iron,
And tethered the hind legs
With silver fetter-locks out of the best silver.

Stretching the silver-bronze reins,
Waving with his black whip,
Flashing with his black eyes,
Handsome Mingian examined with his sharp sight
Surrounding lands by four sides:
Nothing he saw ahead.
Bumba's bright-yellow roof still shone behind.
Disgruntled by the sight, Mingian grumbled:
"Sharga, after three weeks,
We are still at the walls of Bumba.
How long would your leisurely voyage last?"
Golden Sharga grumbled back:
"Bumba's bright-yellow roof is three fingers below the sky.
Bumba shines beyond a three-week journey.
Now, try to stay on my back!
If you, flying over my hindquarters, fall on the ground,
Then blame yourself. You shall not be my rider.
I won't regret leaving you!"

Mingian put away his smoking pipe
And mounted Golden Sharga.
Moving like a storm of thick dust,
As if he was envious of the speed of wind,
Frightened by scattered pebbles and rocks,
Anxious to touch the ashes of earth,
Golden Sharga galloped away.

Seven times seven—forty-nine days,
Sharga flew like a released arrow,
Losing count night after night,
Losing time day after day,
Throwing his rider off the saddle, front and back.
Mingian pulled the silver-bronze reins back,
Moving behind the saddle,
But he lost control of his palomino's speed.
Then he wrapped the reins around his right knee,
But Sharga did not slow down.
The rider wrapped the reins around his left knee,
But the speed did not drop.

Holding the silver-bronze reins,
Mingian pushed himself straight,
But Sharga pulled his rider down to his mane.
Mingian tightened the reins short,
Sharga, shrugging the reins off, soared free.
"My dear Sharga, the destination is close,
Reduce your speed!" Mingian asked his horse,
But Sharga stormed like a moving cloud of dust,
The rider could not see anything front and back.

Suddenly, the silver rays
of light shone though the dust.
There were the guards' rows
of silver spears lined up so tightly,
A needle could not be dropped between the spears.
Kicking the leather stirrups
Seven thousand times silently,
Seven thousand times loudly,
Handsome Mingian attacked,
Jumping on top of the army of spears.

After a fierce fight, Sharga said:
"My Mingian, retreat!
My four black hooves are almost torn out!"
Mingian, turning around, fled.
When they escaped,
Without bending high field grass,
Without waving low field grass,
Sharga glided with a measured pace.
Suddenly, Mingian saw a goddess-faced woman,
Sun and Moon compete with the beauty of her face.
She strolled along the road,
Dressed in many layers of silk dresses,
Covering her long fur lion skin
And swift four-toes gazelle feet.
Mingian greeted her:
"Dear Sister, are you in peace and health?"
Moving her scarlet plump lips,
She did not utter a word, like a fish.

Mingian dismounted, tying his horse to the saddlebow.
He placed a saddle pillow on the ground,
Helped the woman sit on the silver-stitched cushion,
Opened her mouth with the sandalwood whip handle,
And saw two blue needles pierced across her throat.
Clutching the sharp ends with his thumb and index fingers,
Mingian removed the needles.

Passing to her a healing pipe, he asked:
"Whose daughter are you?
What is the name of this land?
Tell me clearly and truthfully!"
The woman smiled, showing her white teeth, and replied:
"Rational words are scarce for true thoughts and intentions.
Passionate words are abundant for our happy life together,
We are destined by the attraction rules of the Universe.
Turk Khan Altan ordered me to report him immediately,
If I see anyone, approaching from the side of the rising sun.
In the middle of the day,
I saw a storming cloud of dust
Forming the horizon that holds the Blue Sky.
A lonely hero was equal to an army
Of ten and hundred thousands.
Who is the mother who gave birth to such a hero-man?
Who is the mare that foaled such a hero-horse?
Hero Mingian,
There is no fire from a single ruby-hot coal,
Nor completeness in a lonely being.
Let us marry and live happily somewhere far away."

Handsome Mingian replied:
"If the Khan's mission,
destined by God Sky Tengri,
is not accomplished,
How can we celebrate and live happily?
Show me the path to Turk Khan Altan.
When I finish the mission,
I will pick you up on the way home."
The woman's feelings oscillated:

"Having a man who asks is bad,
Having no man who asks is bad.
I will show you one path.
If you can follow this path, then go!
If not, stay with me!"
The woman opened the nine layers of dresses
And from the inside pocket of her last dress
Drew a black steel key.
Pointing the key toward the army of spears,
She made a magic unlocking gesture in the air—
Suddenly the path appeared in the wall of spears,
As wide as the eye of the Chinese needle.

Mingian prayed to Bumba's deity-protector.
Mounting, he said to his horse:
"My dear Golden Sharga,
You lead me, I cannot pass through without you!"
He said, releasing the silver-bronze reins.
Tracing the ten-year-old path of a spider,
Tracing the twenty-year-old path of a beetle,
Touching the ground barely with his hooves,
The warrior-horse masterfully passed through the spears.

Seeing the impossible,
The woman pulled violently her lion fur,
Stamped loudly with her four-toes gazelle feet, crying:
"I lost such a beautiful man,
Hoping that he would not go through the given path.
Now, accomplish your mission and return to me!"
Mingian on his Golden Sharga
Passed through the steel spearheads,
Prayed to Bumba's deity-protector,
And galloped away.

Mingian slowed down at the mountain pass,
Stretched the reins and waved with his black whip.
Flashing with his black eyes and sharpening his sight,
Mingian examined the surrounding four sides:
To the north of sunset,

The dark-bronze tower lit like a bonfire from afar.
It must be Turk Khan's palace, Mingian thought.
Mingian descended down the mountain,
And freed Golden Sharga
In the velvet of grasslands
And in the cold of spring waters.
Mingian collected *za*[4]-shrubs,
And starting a campfire,
Boiled a sandalwood red tea.
Then he set up a bright-red tent.
In its shade, stretching out like a resting belt,
Warming up, pink like a *sukha*[5] flower,
He fell into a deep sleep.

Seven times seven, forty-nine days,
Sharga tenderly woke Mingian up, snorting into his face.
Golden Sharga recovered well in the lush pastures.
Mingian turned Golden Sharga
Into a scrubby colt
And himself into a filthy boy—
Ten lice fell
when he scratched his soiled forehead,
Five lice fell
when he scratched his dirty temples.
The filthy boy on his colt Sharga
dab-dab trotted in the outskirts,
Spending a day, where he was given a lunch,
Sleeping overnight,
where he was offered a dinner.

Soon they reached the dark-bronze palace.
The boy freed his colt on the lake pastures,
Put on the black felt coat,
And went to examine the palace city.

4. Saxaul (*Haloxylon aphyllum* Minkw.), the main arboreal cover in the continental steppes of Central Asia; used as firewood by local nomads.

5. Tavolga (*Filipendula rubra*), pink flowers growing in Eastern Siberia, the Far East, and Mongolia.

On the left side of the tower,
Mingian saw Warrior Lanky Tsagan's horse,
As wide as a mountain,
Called Short Shar.
In the morning until noon,
Short Shar was covered with a thick-pile spread,
And with a flat-weave blanket from noon till night.
Mingian listened to many *saaids* discussing:
"Short Shar can catch any horse,
But no horse can catch Short Shar."
Mingian sneaked under the horse,
Examining the horse's teeth, he thought:
This horse can catch my Golden Sharga!

Mingian walked around the palace
Respectfully from left to right,
Found Tengri's son Togya Buse's horse,
Called Black Ermen.
In the morning until noon,
Black Ermen was covered with a thick-pile spread,
And with a flat-weave blanket from noon till night.
The hooves were under a gentle care,
Tied with the soft cotton wrapping.
Mingian listened to many *saaids* discussing:
"After three years of age
A straw-colored falcon with brown streaks
Gains a thin layer of fat on his syncroup
And three fingers of fat under his armpit skin.
As a falcon Black Ermen shall break free,
Soaring high under the bright sun,
Leaving a long train of red dust behind his hooves."
Mingian sneaked under the horse,
Examining the horse teeth, he thought:
This horse can also catch my Golden Sharga!
Other horses next to the palace were not as strong.

Mingian wondered:
In what condition are ten thousand pintos,
Which I shall drive away?

Walking around from the northern side of the palace,
He found the herd that was kept in the stables—
Nine tiers of white strong stone walls,
Nine tiers of black steel gates,
A ninety-nine-spears deep channeled reservoir,
Where the pintos are brought
To drink water only once at noon.
Ten thousand warriors guard the herd day and night.
It seems that the stalls are indestructible.
I will wait for the horses at the water canal at noon,
Mingian thought and went to his Golden Sharga.

Golden Sharga's majestic silver tail rose,
Like a canopy, above his croup:
"You were sent to a foreign land without any knowledge.
What information did you collect?"
Mingian hugged his Sharga around his neck, crying:
"I am sent here alone.
I am not Bumba's scion of legendary families.
I have examined two battle horses.
They can easily catch you, my dear friend!"
Golden Sharga replied:
"We did not come here to collect *edmeg-hermeg*.[6]
We are here to drive away a herd of beautiful horses.
You tell me. Are we here just to look at the horses?
Or are we here to drive them away?
I may not be the fastest horse in the world,
But no horse escapes from my clever tricks."
They decided to develop a plan in the morning
And went to sleep.

When Mingian woke up, he rode on Sharga to the water canal.
Then, he turned Sharga into a femur bat
and himself into a spider with four pairs of legs.
Driving ten thousand pintos
On both sides of the mountain road,

6. *Edmeg*: a cottage cheese–like substance remaining after distilling a milk alcoholic beverage; *hermeg*: sour milk remaining after distilling a milk alcoholic beverage.

The guards brought the herd to the water canal.
Turk Khan's horses drank
Without touching the water with their mouth or hooves.
The battle horses were almost mature,
Growing their hooves into crushing steel,
And their tails and mane into soaring wings.
Moving from the seaside closer to the herd,
Mingian uttered the sounds from a thicket of za-shrubs,
Trembling the continent of Zambu-tiv.
Mingian uttered the sounds from a deep forest,
Trembling the lowland swamps,
Bursting a gallbladder of the old leopard,
Peacefully resting in the desert.
Startled, ten thousand pintos
Straightened their ears, five spans in width,
Crossed their scissor-like ear tips in the middle and
Raised their majestic tails, eighty-eight meters in length.
They crashed one hundred thousand guards
And galloped to the rising sun.

Mingian ran from the seaside to Sharga,
Mounting his horse, he chased the herd,
Making a sound of one hundred thousand galloping army.
Kicking the leather stirrups
Seven thousand times silently,
Seven thousand times loudly,
Mingian summoned and drove the horses,
Turning them into a moving cloud.
The herd was a storm of thick dust.
As if they were envious of the speed of wind,
Frightened by scattered pebbles and rocks,
Anxious to touch the ashes of earth,
Ten thousand pintos sped against the wind,
The wind played with their manes
And tails like strings on a harp.

At that time, Turk Altan was being served
His afternoon tea at the Khan's court.
After two sips, raising a teabowl,

The Khan spilled some tea on the golden tea table.
"Last night in my dream,
I saw a devil riding from the east.
In the morning delight and afternoon indulgence,
I forgot about my dream.
Go outside and look at the sky!"
Khan ordered to his knights.
The knights reported back:
"The sky and the earth are wrapped in a black cloud!"
Turk Khan got up from his golden tea table.
Thirteen palace doors were opened for him.
The Khan went outside,
Looking at the rising sun on the horizon, he ordered:
"Check with the stable guards:
Who is driving my ten thousand pintos
Toward the Khanate of Jangar,
the scion of the Uzunga familial dynasty?"
The stable guards replied:
"It looked like a hundred thousand warriors,
But it was only one man."

Turk Altan Khan further ordered:
"My boars from the Right Wing,
My lions from the Left Wing,
Summon at the Khan's court!"
A thousand white warriors
Arrived at the palace:
"Are we here to catch someone?"
Turk Altan Khan announced:
"Jangar's warrior is driving
My herd of ten thousand pintos.
Bring me that warrior alive!"
Warrior Lanky Tsagan
And Tengri's son Togya Buse
Drank from the yellow porcelain bowls,
Turning them over three times,
One and seventy men
Hardly could raise the bowls together,

And mounting their battle horses, galloped away.

Poor Mingian drove ten thousand pintos,
Directing the herd with his sharp steel spear.
After seven days, in the afternoon,
Turk Khan's two warriors caught up with Mingian.
Drawing out their axes,
They attacked Mingian,
Ready to chop him from left and right.
Yet, Golden Sharga knew many tricks.
When a horse turned once, Sharga could turn seven times.
Golden Sharga raced, saving Mingian
From sharp blades and arrows.
Mingian on his dear Sharga,
Losing count night after night,
Losing time day after day,
Drove ten thousand pintos without a stop.
The chase continued for
Seven times seven—forty-nine days.
First, they passed the Golden Bridge,
Then, they passed the Silver Bridge,
Finally, they saw the bright-yellow palace Bumba from afar.
Golden Sharga said to Mingian:
"Throw your steel spear at one of the knights!"
By the morning, when two knights attacked Mingian,
Golden Sharga, making a sharp turn, escaped the shooting.
Mingian, piercing with his spear,
Raised on the spearhead high above his head
Both Lanky Tsagan and,
As wide as a mountain, his horse Short Shar.
At that minute, Tengri's son Togya Buse
Released his bright-motley whistling arrow
From his intricately decorated blue bow,
As wide as a doorjamb.
Penetrating through Mingian's first thoracic vertebra,
The bright-motley arrow
Got stuck in Sharga's neck.
Mingian with his teeth

Pulled the arrow out of Sharga's neck,
Broke it and spat the broken arrow out.

Chewing the bronze-silver reins,
Horse Black Ermen said to Togya:
"Mingian is not stronger than you, Togya!
Sharga is not faster than me.
Shoot Sharga's four hooves
Before they reach Bumba!"
Sharga sped up,
But could not escape from Togya's arrows.
Golden Sharga cried:
"My dear Mingian,
Your Sharga is shot in four hooves.
I can race until the midday tomorrow.
Then, I will collapse.
You felt that you were alone
Among Jangar's heroes.
You were right.
You are a lonely orphan in Bumba.
You were right.
You are forgotten
Among large familial circles.
Where is Boar who promised
To wait for you at the Golden Bridge?
Where is Lion who promised
To wait for you at the Silver Bridge?"
Next day at noon, Sharga slowed down,
Losing his strength for tricks and race.
Togya Buse threw his axe.
Breaking seventy-two hooks of armor,
The blade hit the back of Mingian's neck.
Mingian's body fell on Sharga's soft mane.
Togya drove his axe out of Mingian's body.
Lanky Tsagan freed himself
From the piercing spear.
Both of them threw Mingian on the ground,
Tying his hands.

Togya mounted Mingian on Sharga facing back
And raced, leading the captives,
Back to Turk Altan Khan.
Lanky Tsagan followed
With a herd of ten thousand pintos.

At that time, Jangar's heroes enjoyed
Drinking *arza* and *horza*
And the multi-tiered palace
Buzzed with excitement.
Suddenly, Shaman Golden Heart
Stood forward, calling:
"Our brother Mingian
Completed his mission in a foreign country.
Chased by two ruthless warriors,
He raced back home,
Crossed the khanate border,
And was captured at the walls of Bumba,
After fighting the battle alone.
What are we going to do?"
From Jangar's Right Wing,
Savar Heavy Arm stood forward:
"Prepare my mare Kurung Galzan!"
From Jangar's Left Wing,
Scarlet Lion Khongor stood forward:
"My stallion is lazy,
But he gets the target.
My stallion is lazy,
But he brings me to the destination.
Prepare my Lazy Galzan!"

Savar and Khongor drank
From two yellow porcelain bowls,
Turning the bowls over three times,
One and seventy men
Hardly could raise them together.
They put on their battle armor.
Khongor attached his bright-motley lance.
Savar put over his shoulder

His twelve-blades axe.
Savar and Khongor raced shoulder to shoulder,
Singing harmoniously a beautiful song.
Savar Heavy Arms said to his mare:
"Were not you a foal,
Whom I bought for a million smokes?[7]
By the first ray of the morning sun
Catch Togya Buse
Before he enters the Golden Bridge!
If you won't deliver me on time,
Your croup hide will cover the drum,
Eight ribs of yours will be the drumsticks,
Four hooves will be useful as candleholders!"
Pledging, Savar licked his sacred axe.
"Listen! Until the dawn,
Manage to stay on my back.
If you, flying over my croup,
Fall on the ground,
Then blame yourself.
You shall not be my rider.
I won't regret leaving you!"
Mare Kurung Galzan replied
And flew with the speed of wind.

By sunrise, Savar on Kurung Galzan caught up
with Togya Buse right before the Golden Bridge.
Togya Buse turned around—
Savar's black axe was alive in flame.
Releasing Sharga's reins,
Togya raced to the Golden Bridge.
Riding behind Togya,
Savar stood on the stirrups
And hit the back of Togya's neck with his axe,
Breaking fifty hooks of armor.
Togya lost his consciousness and,
Closing his bright-black eyes,

7. The basis of the census: one smoke comes from one tent or household.

Fell on Black Ermen's soft mane.
Savar's axe broke with the blades
Trapped in Togya's back.
Savar pulled Togya's coat hem from the back,
Pushed him on Black Ermen's croup,
Wide as an anvil,
And tying his arms and legs with the blue silk straps,
Secured him to the saddlebow.
Pulling Ermen's silver reins,
Savar trotted to find Khongor.

Red Lion Khongor,
Right next to the Silver Bridge,
Raised Lanky Tsagan on his bright-motley spearhead,
Raced back from the Silver Bridge.

Summoning ten thousand pintos,
They galloped to their friend Mingian.
Dismounting, two heroes embraced Mingian, crying:
"We forgot about you not because you are alone,
nor because you are without your ancient roots.
Drinking *arza* and *horza*,
We lost the passing of time
in the multi-tiered palace buzzed with excitement."
They sent ahead Togya Buse and Lanky Tsagan
And following the herd,
Losing count night after night,
Raced without a stop to Bumba.
Soon they reached the bright-yellow Bumba Tower.
They dismounted, tying their horses to the saddlebow,
Ringing the bells, opened the jade-silver palace door,
And bowing to the throne three times,
Sat at their positions.

When the guards unlocked the captives' fetters,
Togya Buse and Lanky Tsagan
Stepped offensively on ten *saaids*,
Slapped boisterously five *saaids*,
Sat in the middle of the court hall,

Saying to the Great Khan Jangar:
"We shall defend you in wars,
Supply you with the battle horses,
And enter the Khanate of Bumba."
Jangar replied:
"Why are you asking me? You shall ask my twelve boars,
Whose bodies were tempered in the flame of wars,
Whose fame was spread in the near lands and far away."

Savar Heavy Arm, a human falcon,
Stood forward on behalf of the boars,
Slapping poor Togya and Tsagan
with the stamped act of surrender he said:
"Under the order of the Great Khan Jangar,
Turk Altan's Khanate is subject to Bumba!
You are expected to submit an annual tribute!"
Savar announced the order and let Togya and Tsagan free,
Sending ten thousand pintos back to Turk Altan Khan.
Since that time,
The enlightened lord Jangar
United the four truths with his own hands,
The statehood he created was indestructible,
The glory was uncontrollable,
Rattling beyond his spacious land.
In bliss and peace,
Bumba of wise Jangar spectacularly shone.

"If she looked to the left, the radiance on her left cheek made the little fish visible in the river on the left."

How Mingian, the Finest Man in the Universe, Captured Mighty Kurmen Khan

Six thousand and twelve heroes,
Scions of legendary families,
Sat in seven circles in the court hall.
Milk from the wild steppe mares
Formed overflowing rivers,
Arza from the wild mares
Formed overflowing lakes.
When the multi-tiered palace
Buzzed with excitement,
Jangar Khan tried to hide clear tears
Falling from his sad eyes,
Wiping them left and right
With his black silk robe sleeves.
Many *saaids* noticed his tears.
Turning to Eloquent Mediator Jilgan,
They offered him a bowl of *arza,* saying:
"Have a drink first and then ask the Khan about his distress."

Eloquent Mediator Jilgan
Three times drank from a yellow
Porcelain bowl,
Seventy men hardly could raise it together.
Three times bowed
His black head to Buddhas.

He stretched his arms wide,
Opened his dark-red palms up to the sky,
Kneeled on the silver-hemmed fluffy fur blanket and said:
"Great Khan Jangar,
Perhaps, you feel sad
Because your five-year-old Aranzal,
Foaled from the famous maiden mare,
Is not as fast as before.
Perhaps, you feel sad
Because your bright-yellow lance
Is not as sharp as before.
Perhaps, you feel sad
Because your Shavdal Khatun
Is not as gentle as before.
Perhaps, you feel sad
Because Bumba's population
In seventy khanates,
Swirling like a heavy cloud,
Swarming like an ant colony,
Is not large enough.
Perhaps, you feel sad
Because six thousand and twelve heroes
Are not as capable as before.
Perhaps, you feel sad
Because Bumba palace,
Ten tiers high and nine colors bright,
Is not marvelous enough.
Please share your private pain with us!"

Wiping his pure *arshan* tears with the fresh yellow scarf,
Jangar Khan opened up to numerous *saaids:*
"Content with all that I have,
I am saddened by the grave threat.
Happy today, we may not be tomorrow.
Mighty Khan Kurmen, who conquered Uzunga,
Lives to the north of sunset.
In envy, he said:
'In charge of the khanate of the rising sun is an orphan.

He is the only son of Uzunga Khan, whom I conquered.
The statehood he created is indestructible,
The glory is uncontrollable,
Rattling beyond Bumba's spacious land.'
Kurmen Khan prepares to send an envoy to Bumba.
We must capture Kurmen Khan before he sends his envoy!"
Shaman Golden Heart said:
"Great Khan Jangar,
You foresaw the consequences of this military strategy.
You must choose the hero for this adventure."

Jangar Khan turned to Mingian:
"My dear Mingian,
The most handsome man in the Universe,
Among the six thousand and twelve strongest boars of
    Bumba,
Are you not one of the best heroes?
Is your horse Golden Sharga not tempered in the war
    flames?
Is he not half a *beeria* faster than the speed of thought,
One *beeria* faster than the speed of wind?
Bring me Kurmen Khan alive!"

Mingian sat in front with pure *arshan* tears
Rolling down his cheeks:
"Jangar, my dear Khan,
Named after Mingi Mountain,
Was not I the Khan
Of the Mingi Mountain Khanate,
The Khan of ten million people,
The Khan of my own land?
After fighting with us for three weeks,
Did not you leave without a victory?
When you left with your boars,
Looking at you from the distance
Of three miles,
I saw that you were destined to become
The conqueror of all under the sun.
I relinquished my Mingi Mountain Khanate

And leadership over ten million subjects.
I left my fair-face *khatun*
And my cute daughter with rosy cheeks.
Did not I follow you on my Golden Sharga,
Giving up everything that was dear to me,
Changing my khan status
To the title *sengche*
If so, why are you sending me alone
Against the colossal enemy?
Are you targeting me
Because I am rootless in Bumba?
Are you not targeting the *saaids*
Because their familial trees
Are rooted here deep and tight?
Before I race to the foreign land,
I have no sister to spoil me
With a delightful meal
From the familial cauldron,
I have no brother to miss me
At home when I am away."
Mingian sat sad with falling tears.

Shaman Golden Heart interfered:
"Oh, my dear friend Mingian,
You are a respected man in any khanate in the world.
If you accomplish the operation, it would be a heroic deed.
If not, Kurmen Khan would offer you
the same position *sengche,* fear not!"

After these encouraging words,
Mingian drank from a yellow porcelain bowl,
Turning it over seventy-one times,
Seventy men hardly could raise it together.
His heated heart exhilarated,
Boiling twelve courages inside,
Ready to break out of his chest cage.
His ten white fingers squeezed into menacing fists.
Handsome Mingian roared:
"If my dried body gets lost,

Earth will benefit from a handful of ashes!
If my wounded body gets lost,
Earth will benefit from a bowl of blood!
Bring me my Golden Sharga!"
A devoted horse-breeder ran outside.
In the cold of spring waters,
In the velvet of grasslands,
Among the countless racehorses,
Among the dark herds,
The palomino stallion frolicked and played.
The horse-breeder mounted Golden Sharga,
And moving clockwise from left to right,
Made an honorable canter around the palace.
Then he fastened the horse's slender forelegs
With hobbles out of the best iron,
And tethered the hind legs
With fetter-locks out of the best silver.
He pulled the horse with fifty *saaids*' sons,
And brought Golden Sharga to the front gate.
On a saddletree panel,
Decorated with silver plaques,
Over a six-layered saddle blanket,
As spacious as a steppe,
He placed a saddle, as large as an anvil.
Wide and comfortable,
It looked like a canyon.
The saddle was covered with a pillow
Adorned with Tibetan silver.
Along the patterned fenders,
Between the horse's prolonged ribs,
Through the eighty fine silver rings,
The horse-breeder pulled the leather straps.
When he fastened the girds so firmly,
Sweat and lather released
From the eighty fine silver rings.
When he secured the straps so tight,
The horse's belly tightened seventy-two layers of fat.

Golden Sharga's sacrum was divine—
The beauty of his power
Was concentrated in his sacrum.
There was sharp precision in his expressive eyes
And rapid speed in his swift feet.
Golden Sharga played
with the moon and the sun,
Catching their rays
in his thick velvet mane.
He rattled his armor,
Imagining that his four hooves
Were tramping the enemy's land.
The palomino stallion
Leaped upward and forward,
Throwing *saaids'* sons to one corner,
Throwing *saaids'* sons to the other corner.

Handsome Mingian put on
A pair of blood-red fine-leather boots—
No better boots will ever
Be found in the world!
One hundred ladies sewed the soles;
One thousand ladies stitched
The bootleg lining.
Had you seen the footprint
of the boots alone,
You would offer
One thousand coins for them;
After seeing this masterwork on Mingian
You would give ten thousand.
Over a gauzy silk undershirt and three precious robes
He put on his unique battle armor.
Over a silk sash, he fastened an iron belt
Equal in cost to seventy horses.
Mingian grasped a whip in his grip.
The core was plaited
With three-year-old bull leather,
The surface was made

Of four-year-old bull hide.
Designed as patterns
On the back of a snake,
Boiled in the saliva of a snake,
Soaked in the poison of a snake—
The treated whip was famous for its strength.
A steel plate was at the end of the whip;
When it whips, it burns like fire.
Its sandalwood handle had, at its end,
A wrist loop made of scarlet red silk.
Mingian attached his yellow sword to the iron belt.
Ready on the right side to swing and strike,
It was seventy and one *ald* in length.

Handsome Mingian, bending his knee, bowed to the throne.
Mingian walked, pressing the coral path
With his red soft leather boots,
Pushing the jade-silver shutter doors,
Ringing the door bells, he went outside the palace.
Mingian mounted his horse, hardly touching the stirrup;
The toe of his blood-red fine-leather boot moved
As swift as a ruby coal bouncing off fire.
Six thousand and twelve heroes recited a poem-*magtal*
Wishing Mingian success in his journey
And safe return back to the jade-silver gates of Bumba.
Holding gracefully the silver-bronze reins in his hands,
Moving respectfully clockwise from left to right
Mingian made an elegant canter around the palace,
And galloped away toward the sunset.

At the mountain observation post Bolzatin Boro,
Mingian dismounted, tying his horse to the saddlebow,
Lay down on the ground and wept.
Shaman Golden Heart followed Mingian,
Racing on his battle horse Aksak Ulan.
His black cape floated magnificently in the wind.
When Shaman Golden Heart found Mingian,
He kneeled next to him, saying:
"Oh, poor Mingian, come here!"

Shaman put Mingian's head on the right knee,
Kissing his right cheek.
Shaman turned Mingian's head on the left knee,
Kissing his left cheek and said:
"I came here, my dear Mingian,
To show the path in your adventure.
After three months of your journey,
You shall meet a ferocious beast—
Tengri's white camel Khavshil.[1]
Gnashing his teeth in rage,
Khavshil ignites twelve flames of fire.
But you are smarter than Khavshil, use your tricks!

"After three more months,
In the shade of three magic sandal and poplar trees,
You shall meet five hundred maiden-witches.
Do not look straight at their eyes!
Golden lassos are hidden in their delightful mouths.
Behind their divine lips are traps.
Release your horse's reins,
Golden Sharga shall safely lead you out of this place.
After three more months,
You shall meet two vicious gadflies in the steppe.
Again, release your horse's reins,
Golden Sharga shall safely lead you out of this place.
Soon you shall meet Kurmen's Khatun's maid.
Born as a princess,
She is a relative of Jangar Khan.
Befriend the lady.
She shall help you in this adventure."
Shaman recited a poem of blessing
Wishing Mingian success in his journey
And safe return back
To the jade-silver gates of Bumba.
Mounting Aksak Ulan,

---

1. Khavshil: specifically, a male camel when he ferociously gnashes his teeth to assert dominance.

Shaman galloped toward the sunrise.

Mingian on Golden Sharga
Galloped away toward the sunset,
Kicking the leather stirrups
Seven thousand times silently,
Seven thousand times loudly.
A leap of Sharga's hind legs
Covers the distance of one day;
A jump of his front legs
Covers the distance of two days.
Golden Sharga's chest supported his chin,
When he dived,
Touching the black soil with his chin,
He snorted fire,
Burning the grass into ashes.
Then, he soared like a white hare,
Gently brushing the young grass fields.

Three months have passed.
Suddenly, Golden Sharga halted
From the teeth-grinding screech.
Tengri's white camel Khavshil, igniting a fire,
Shot twelve flames at Mingian from afar.
Mingian dismounted,
Tying his horse to the saddlebow,
And ran to White Khavshil
With a black whip in his fist.
Tengri's White Khavshil
Almost caught him on the right.
Then, Mingian jumped
From the left side on the camel,
Mounting between two humps.
White Khavshil pulled him
From left and right,
But Mingian evaded the camel's attacks.
Drawing his sharp yellow sword out,
Mingian knocked out the camel's brain.
When White Khavshil fell on the ground,

Ninety-nine rivers extended the flows.
Mingian cut, cooked,
And ate two humps and,
Mounting Golden Sharga,
He prayed to Bumba's deities and
Galloped without a stop for three months.

In the shade of three magic sandal and poplar trees,
Five hundred maiden-witches approached Mingian.
Offering him drinks and delights
With ninety-nine hidden spells,
They lured him, singing:
"Our honorable brother
Might be thirsty and hungry."
Enchanted with sweet maiden voices,
Recalling barely Shaman's words,
Mingian released the silver-bronze reins.
Freed, palomino Golden Sharga
Straightening his ears,
Six spans in width,
Jumped in the air eighteen thousand times,
Landed on the ground
Eighteen thousand times.
As if he was frightened
By scattered pebbles under his hooves,
Golden Sharga, evading the maidens,
Galloped away.
Five hundred witches cried,
Covering their mouth
From surprise and frustration:
"We lured hundred-thousands without a combat,
We lured ten-thousands without a delay.
We missed a great warrior.
Let's wish him to safely complete his task and
Meet him again on the way back."
Mingian prayed to Bumba's deities and
Galloped without a stop for three months.

Suddenly, a hazy rain *byur-byur* drizzled,

A blowing wind *sab-sab* drubbed.
Two black heavy clouds, blown by the wind,
Circled above Mingian's head.
Following Shaman's advice,
Mingian released the reins,
Praying to Bumba's deities.
Two gadflies flew out of the clouds, ready to sting Mingian.
When Sharga jumped in the air eighteen thousand times,
Two gadflies attacked from below.
When Sharga landed on the ground eighteen thousand times,
Two gadflies attacked from above.
Soon, the tormentors could fly no more,
Dropping flat on their yellow bellies,
Shivering frantically on the ground.
Mingian pulled the silver-bronze reins,
And turned Sharga around,
He cut and burnt the defeated gadflies.
Happy Mingian felt reassured:
"Now, three threats are behind,
Thanks to Uncle Shaman."
Mingian prayed to Bumba's deities and
Galloped without a stop for seven days.

Mingian slowed down
At Ole Manghan Tsagan Mount,
Stretched the silver-bronze reins
And waved with his black whip.
Flashing with his black eyes,
He examined the surrounding lands by four sides:
On the west, the castle gloomily rose,
Shaped as a *garuda*,[2] made of glass.
How is this palace compared with Jangar's Bumba?
He wondered.
The palace was five fingers wider and reached the sky.
The Khan of this palace, perhaps, is the lord
Of one of the four sides of the world,

2. Eagle.

As happy as Jangar the Great.
It would be impossible to enter this palace!
Mingian cried with tears as clear as *arshan*.

Mingian descended down the mountain,
And freed Golden Sharga
In the velvet of grasslands
And in the cold of spring waters.
Mingian collected *za*-shrubs,
And starting a campfire,
Boiled the sandalwood red tea.
Then he set up a bright-red tent.
In its shade, stretching out like a resting belt,
Warming up, pink like a *sukha* flower,
He fell into a deep sleep.

Seven times seven, forty-nine days,
Sharga tenderly woke Mingian up, snorting into his face.
Golden Sharga recovered well in the lush pastures.
Mingian turned Golden Sharga into a shabby colt
And himself into a filthy boy—
Ten lice fell when he scratched his soiled forehead,
Five lice fell when he scratched his dirty temples.
The filthy boy on his colt Sharga
Dab-dab trotted on the outskirts,
Spending a day, where he was given a lunch,
Sleeping overnight, where he was offered a dinner.

One evening, they reached the outskirts of the palace city.
A maiden from the Garuda-Eagle Tower,
As beautiful as the moon and the sun,
Approached the boy.
When the boy turned,
She turned following him.
When the boy walked faster,
She sped up too.
Facing the little boy, she addressed him:
"Honorable Knight!
Wishing you an eternal peace!"

Trembling with anger, the boy replied:
"Have you lost your mind from your idle palace life?
Your mockery is useless here.
If you need a grown-up for your foolish jokes,
Go and find a *tsakhar* good fellow!"
The young lady smiled:
"I recognized you.
From the northeast,
Jangar Khan sent you, Mingian,
Erke Tug Khan's son,
The most handsome man in the Universe.
Do not hide from me, I shall help you!"
"You are right.
I am Mingian, son of Erke Tug Khan.
On behalf of Jangar Khan,
I am here to capture Kurmen Khan alive.
What would be your advice?"
"You know about me
from Shaman Golden Heart.
Kurmen is the Khan
Of one of the four khanates of the world.
White Old Sage, the lord of the world,
Is his God protector.
In the dusk, White Old Sage appeared,
Warning Kurmen:
'From the sunrise,
Jangar Khan's devil has arrived!'
Kurmen Khan ignored the warning:
'Impossible—there is no threat
from the lands of Uzunga,
whom I conquered before!
You knew the future in the past;
You knew the past in the future;
But, I see, you have become old;
The gold of your prophecy no longer shines.'

"When I heard these words,
I came here to meet you.

Kurmen Khan always wears a white amulet on his neck.
Under a spell of the amulet,
the Khan has been undefeated.
Without the white amulet on his neck,
Kurmen is strong as a child.
Honorable Mingian,
Tonight, when the guards are asleep,
Turning Shraga into a sheep-bone[3] at the gate,
Enter the palace,
Taking the amulet off his neck, capture Kurmen Khan!
If you fail the task,
Bow before the Khan in the morning,
Be Kurmen Khan's best *sengche!*"
After meeting with Mingian,
The young lady returned to the palace.

At midnight, Mingian turned himself
Into a venomous snake.
Bending his spine into serpentine coils,
Mingian moved fast, passing
Eight thousand guards outside the palace,
Eight thousand guards inside the palace.
Then, leaving a sheep-bone, Sharga,
At the silver-jade shutter gate,
Crawling through the cracks of fourteen doors,
Mingian emerged in the *torlok* court hall
And sat on the right side from the doorstep.
In the dim light of the high white lantern,
Kurmen slept on the white sacred throne,
Holding his yellow steel sword on his chest.
Next to him, a leopard and a bear rested,
Ready to tear apart and throw the intruder
To the left and right dungeons of hell.
Mingian trembled with fear.
Red marrow panged in his eight long bones,

---

3. *Shagai*: astragalus sheep-bone, used for throwing games, board games, and fortune-telling.

Tears pure as *arshan* rolled down his cheeks.

Turning into a spider
With four pairs of legs,
The young lady removed
The amulet off Kurmen's neck
And hung it on Mingian's neck, saying:
"I put the leopard and the bear to sleep
For seven times seven—forty-nine days.
Mounting Golden Sharga,
I will fight with eighteen thousand internal guards.
When you finish your task,
Meet me outside at the first light of dawn."
When the lady left,
Mingian drank from a yellow porcelain bowl,
Turning it over seventy-one times,
One and seventy men hardly could raise it together.
At last, the knight's throat warmed up from drinking,
His heated heart exhilarated,
Boiling twelve courages inside,
Ready to break out of his chest cage.
His ten white fingers squeezed into menacing fists.
His sharp black eyes
Rolled in the eye sockets twelve times,
Adjusting the vision into the precision
Of an attacking falcon.
Mingian bowed three times
And turned off the white lantern.
He grabbed Kurmen's yellow sword and,
Raising it above his body, exclaimed:
"I am not the one who is raising his hand.
Jangar Khan is raising his hand!"
Mingian stabbed Kurmen with the sword,
Turning it in his stomach seventy-one times.
Kurmen Khan jumped on his feet
and threw Mingian to the right dungeon of hell.
But clever Mingian on the pinky toe of his right foot
Resisted the fall and jumped back on his feet.

Kurmen Khan threw Mingian to the left dungeon of hell.
But clever Mingian on the pinky toe of his left foot
Resisted the fall and jumped back on his feet.
Mingian, grappling the Khan,
Threw him at the throne with all his might.
Tying Kurmen's hands and feet together
Behind his back as wide as an anvil,
Mingian put Kurmen in the yellow sack,
Threw it over his shoulder,
Pushing fourteen shutter doors went outside.

Through the night till the first faint ray of dawn,
The lady-warrior on Golden Sharga
Battled against eighteen thousand internal guards.
Mingian, jumping over three thousand heads,
Landed on the saddle pillow
Adorned with Tibetan silver.
Turning into a bright-yellow silk scarf,
The lady-warrior tacked behind his sash.
Mingian galloped away,
Kicking the leather stirrups
Seven thousand times silently,
Seven thousand times loudly.
A leap of Sharga's hind legs covers the distance of one day;
A jump of his forelegs covers the distance of two days.
Sharga's chest supported his chin,
When he dived, touching the black soil with his chin,
He snorted fire, burning the grass into ashes.
Black dust fell behind his hooves,
Swirling into clouds, reaching the sky.
Altan Sharga threw his rider off the saddle, front and back.
Freeing himself from the grip of the silver-bronze reins.

The lady-warrior decided to cover
the nine-months distance within nine days.
She channeled the heated wind,
Blowing behind Sharga's majestic tail,
Eighty-eight *ald* in length.
Five days have passed.

Warrior Leopard Mergen,
Riding Shar Tsokhor with a short-cut tail,
Caught up with Mingian.
The lady-warrior shouted:
"Mingian, give me your blue bow, as wide as a doorjamb.
If Leopard Mergen's collar is unbuttoned, we will be lucky.
If not, we shall lose this fight!"
Drawing a bow, she released the arrow.
Leopard Mergen's collar
Was opened from the heat,
With two undone buttons.
The arrow propelled straight
Into Leopard Mergen's neck,
Smashing his head.
His horse Shar Tsokhor
Raced to save his master.
But the lady-warrior,
Jumping on the ground,
Pulled Shar Tsokhor
By the bright-yellow halters
And wrapped the silver reins
Around her knee.
She thrust the sword deep
In the ground and,
Holding the sword
from being dragged by the horse,
Halted the battle horse Shar Tsokhor.
At that moment, Leopard Mergen's spirit departed his body.

Mingian, turning Golden Sharga
Around, dismounted.
Removing Leopard Mergen's battle armor,
He quickly chopped and burnt the dead body,
Preventing Leopard Mergen's
Magical recovery.
Taking with him
The battle horse Shar Tsokhor,
Mingian on his dear Golden Sharga

Galloped away.

On the ninth day, Mingian
Made an honorable canter
Around the bright-yellow Bumba palace
And dismounted at the silver-jade gate.
Twelve senior *saaids*
Opened the yellow sack,
Unlocked Kurmen's fetters, saying:
"You are invited to sit
On the right side from Jangar Khan,
On the throne with eight legs out of pure silver."
Kurmen Khan, ignoring the *saaids,*
Sat above Jangar Khan's seat.
For seven times seven—forty-nine days,
In the feast of the feast,
They all drank *arza* together.
Kurmen Khan stood forward, announcing:
"Son of Great Khan Uzunga,
The only scion of the ancient dynasty,
Jangar, rule your nation!"
Accompanied by twelve senior *saaids,*
Kurmen Khan went outside and galloped back home.

The multi-tiered palace
Buzzed with excitement.
In the middle of the feast,
Shaman Golden Heart interfered loudly:
"My dear Mingian,
Please show us your gorgeous
Bright-yellow silk scarf,
Tacked behind your sash and silver belt!"
When Mingian pulled out the scarf,
The scarf turned into a gorgeous lady,
Beaming with the light of many stars.
When she sat next to Shavdal Khatun,
Her energy shone brighter
than Khatun's beauty.
"An extraordinary goddess

Shall be matched with an extraordinary man,
Such as Mingian!" everyone sighed in awe.
"No," replied Mingian.
"Her merits are greater than mine.
She is more than a wife.
I owe her my life."
Among six thousand twelve heroes
A match was found,
Alia Shonkhor, son of Shaman Golden Heart.
The palace buzzed with excitement.
Milk from the wild steppe mares
Formed overflowing rivers,
Arza from the wild mares
Formed overflowing lakes.
Pleasing and tempting to merrymaking.
The feasts lasted long.
The drinking lasted long.

How Serious Sanal Defeated the Country of Half-Human Giants

Six thousand and twelve heroes,
Scions of legendary families,
Sat in seven circles in the court hall.
Slowly examining his heroes, Jangar
Selected Sanal:
"Serious Sanal, Bulingir's son.
Kyuder Khan, whom I want to send you to,
Controls the distant foreign lands.
Deliver him my message:
If he wants peace,
Listen to his conditions of peace.
If he wants war,
Listen to his conditions of war."

Serious Sanal took his golden helmet off,
Sat in front of Jangar,
Bowed to the throne three times,
And said with his *arshan* tears
Rolling down the cheeks:
"Jangar the Khan,
Following you, the Conqueror of the World,
I left behind my father Bulingir.
My father was deprived
Of the presence of his dear son.

Glorious and noble,
Equal to Buddhas themselves,
My mother was deprived
Of the wake memorials made by her son.
In my rich country
No man could replace my noble position.
My beautiful wife Angira was deprived
Of my marriage and love.
Before I race to the foreign land,
Neither a sister spoils me with a delightful meal,
Cooked in the ancestral cauldron,
Nor a brother stays behind
To miss me at home.
Dear Jangar Khan, send your lions
Who are stronger than I."

Great Khan Jangar leaned forward and said,
Brushing Sanal's silver curves back
With his ten white fingers:
"You are not alone.
Don't be afraid of many enemies.
Convey the message and come back!
If Kyuder Khan wishes peace,
Secure his three pledges of alliance,
Military service for fifty years,
And taxes for one and thousand years.
If Kyuder Khan declares war,
Rip his black banner and
Bring it to me with his
Eighty thousand piebald stallions!

When Sanal returned to his seat,
Jangar asked Shaman:
"Shaman Golden Heart,
How far is Kyuder's Khanate?"
Shaman reported to Jangar:
"Kyuder's Khanate
Is southwest of here.
If you send a three-year-old straw saker,

With a thin layer of fat on her syncroup
And three fingers of fat under her wing,
In her journey, she would lay eggs
And hatch chicks three times,
But still would not reach the khanate.
If you send a common stallion,
He would race for forty-nine months,
But still would not reach the khanate.
Khan Kyuder sits in his palace and drinks *arza*
With one hundred thousand fair heroes,
Urging them to add
To three conquered khanates of the world
The last missing khanate,
The eastern Khanate of Jangar."

After hearing the words of threat to Bumba,
Sanal drank from a yellow porcelain bowl,
Turning it over seventy-one times,
Seventy men hardly could raise it together.
His heated heart exhilarated,
Boiling twelve courages inside,
Ready to break out of his chest cage.
His ten white fingers squeezed
Into menacing fists, as he roared:
"If my dried body is lost,
Earth will benefit from a handful of ashes!
If my wounded body is lost,
Earth will benefit from a bowl of blood!"

Shaman Golden Heart said:
"I always thought that Sanal is the most
Capable nobleman for any challenge.
He is as wise as I, Shaman Golden Heart.
Masterful with his axe as Savar Heavy Arm,
Brave as the leading lion among all lions,
Scarlet Lion Khongor,
Well educated and sophisticated as the most
Handsome man in the world, Mingian.
He is an accomplished nobleman

With ninety-nine virtuous traits.
At last, Sanal's throat
Warmed up from drinking.
His sharp black eyes rolled
In the eye sockets twelve times,
Adjusting his vision
Into the perception of an attacking falcon.
"Bring me my stallion Burul Galzan!"
Sanal ordered.
An assigned horse-breeder
From the khanate stables ran outside.
In the cold of spring waters,
In the velvet of grasslands,
Among the countless racehorses,
Among the dark herds,
The stallion frolicked and played.
The horse-breeder mounted Burul Galzan,
And moving clockwise from left to right,
Made an elegant canter around the palace.
He fastened the horse's slender forelegs
With iron hobbles out of the best iron,
And tethered the hind legs with silver
Fetter-locks out of the best silver.
He pulled the horse
With fifty *saaids*' sons,
And brought the horse to the front gate.
On a saddletree panel,
Decorated with silver plaques,
Over a six-layered saddle blanket,
As spacious as a steppe,
He placed a saddle, as large as an anvil.
Wide and comfortable,
It looked like a canyon.
The saddle was covered with a pillow
Adorned with Tibetan silver.
Along the patterned fenders,
Between the horse's prolonged ribs,
Through the eighty fine silver rings,

The horse-breeder
Pulled the leather straps.
When he fastened the girds so firmly,
Sweat and lather released
From the eighty fine silver rings.
When he secured the straps so tight,
The horse's belly tightened
Seventy-two layers of fat.

Burul Galzan's croup was divine—
The beauty of his power
Was concentrated in his croup.
There was sharp precision in his expressive eyes
And rapid speed in his swift feet.
Burul Galzan played
With the moon and the sun,
Catching their rays
In his thick velvet mane.
He rattled his armor,
Imagining that his four hooves
Were tramping the enemy's land.
The stallion leaped upward and forward,
Throwing the *saaids'* sons to one corner,
Throwing the *saaids'* sons
To the other corner.
Savar Heavy Arm stood forward
and offered Sanal, the son of Bulingir,
His legendary twelve-blades axe.
Tempered in the flames of fights,
Ready to swing and whack,
It was eighty and one meters in length.
"This weapon will help you
In the faraway land," Savar said.
Scarlet Lion Khongor stood forward
and offered Sanal, the son of Bulingir,
His legendary yellow steel sword.
Tempered in the flames of fights,
Ready to swing and strike,

It was seventy-one meters in length.
"This weapon will help you
In the faraway land.
Carry it always on the right side,"
Khongor said.
Fat Belly Gumbe stood forward
And offered Sanal, the son of Bulingir,
His legendary black dagger Khara-Kandzhal.[1]
"This weapon will help you
In the faraway land.
Carry it always on the left side,"
Fat Belly said.

Excited, Sanal grasped a whip in his grip.
Its core was plaited
With three-year-old bull leather;
Its surface
Was made of four-year-old bull hide.
Resembling patterns on the back of a snake,
Boiled in the saliva of a snake,
Soaked in the poison of a snake—
The treated whip
Was legendary for its strength.
A steel plate was at its end;
When it whips, it burns like fire.
A sandalwood handle had, at its end,
A wrist loop made of scarlet red silk.
He clutched the whip so tight,
The released moisture marked the grip.

Jangar the Khan and his heroes
Recited a poem of blessing
Wishing Sanal success in his journey
And safe return back
To the jade-silver gates of Bumba.
Sanal bade farewell and walked outside,
Pressing the coral path

---

1. Name meaning "black dagger"; still used in the Caucasus and Central Asia.

With his red soft leather boots.
The Earth felt heavy
From his sturdy footsteps.
The horsemen led Sanal to Burul Galzan
And helped him to mount his stallion.
Hardly touching a stirrup
With his blood-red fine boot toe,
Sanal mounted his horse,
Hardly touching the stirrup;
The toe of his blood-red
Fine-leather boot moved
As swift as a ruby coal bouncing off fire.
Holding gracefully
The silver reins in his hands,
Moving traditionally clockwise
From left to right,
Sanal made an elegant canter
Around the palace
and galloped away to the southwest.

Jangar with his twelve boars-heroes walked
To the Bumba temple on the oceanfront
And ordered a special service
For Sanal's safe journey.
Then they climbed up
the Manghan Tsagan Mount,
Wondering how far Sanal was riding.
Sanal's silhouette
Was lost beyond the realm.

Three months have passed.
Suddenly, Sanal saw a goddess-faced woman,
Strolling along the road.
Sun and Moon compete
With the beauty of her face.
Offering him drinks and delights
With ninety-nine hidden spells,
She lured him, singing:
"My noble brother might be

Thirsty and hungry."
Sanal cooled his excitement at heart
And cleared his mind, thinking:
Why is she offering me the delicacies
Here, in the middle of nowhere?
She must be a witch.
"Honorable knight,
Dismount and taste my food," she begged.
"Dear sister, I must make haste.
On the way back, I will definitely taste,"
He replied.
"At least, touch the food," she insisted.
Sanal sped, leaving her screaming:
"How dare you refuse me?
When I stab you with my black steel beak
And suck blood out of your heart,
You shall regret!" She chased him.

Sanal galloped away,
Kicking the leather stirrups
Seven thousand times silently,
Seven thousand times shouting loudly.
A leap of Burul Galzan's hind legs
Covered the distance of one day;
A jump of his forelegs
Covered the distance of two days.
Burul Galzan's chest supported his chin,
When he dived,
Touching the black soil with his chin,
He snorted fire,
Burning the grass into ashes.

Escaping the witch,
Burul raced for seven days,
And three times seven days more.
Then he galloped for another three weeks.
Seven times seven—
Forty nine days have passed,
But the witch's beak was still behind,

Nearly catching Burul's majestic tail,
Eighty-eight meters in length.
Burul Galzan called his friend:
"I cannot race faster, my Sanal.
You must do something!"
Sanal drew out Lion Khongor's yellow sword,
Seventy-one meters in length,
Slid down Burul's croup and
Shattered the witch's beak with one thrust.
Pulling the silver reins,
Sanal turned around,
Cut the body and scattered the remnants,
Averting the witch's revival.
Then, mounting his horse,
Sanal galloped to the southwest.

Three months have passed.
Sanal saw a goddess-faced lady,
Approaching him on a piebald stallion.
Sun and Moon compete
With the beauty of her face.
As she was passing, the lady
Pulled the golden reins to the right
And bowed to Sanal's left stirrup,
greeting him:
"Distinguished nobleman,
Wishing you health!"
Sanal was frightened:
"In this desolate and barren steppe,
If I open my mouth to utter a word,
I may lose my tongue."
He ignored her repeated greetings
Three times.
Then, Sanal pulled the yellow steel
Sword out, confronting her:
"Lady, are you here with peace or war?"
"I am the youngest daughter-princess
From a small island Tib,

I am here with a humble request.
Recently, Kyuder Khan's envoy
Came to our country,
Took my brother-prince to his khanate
And threw him into the dungeon.
My uncle shaman said:
'Khan of the eastern side of the world,
the only scion of Uzunga,
Sent a powerful envoy to destroy
Kyuder's army of half-human *mangas*.
We must ask him to save our prince.
If we send a man to meet him,
The fierce envoy would crush the stranger.
Instead, a beautiful goddess
Should meet him,
Offer him drinks and food,
And tell him about our misfortune.'
So, they sent me to graciously greet you.
Be benevolent to us, dear brother,
Accept our feast in the palace,
Raise a bowl of *araka* with us!"
Princess asked with tears, clear as *arshan*,
Rolling down her beautiful cheeks.

Sanal agreed and raced with the princess
To the white palace.
In front of the palace,
They dismounted,
Tied their horses to the saddlebows.
Sanal, ringing the bells,
Pushed the jade-silver shutter doors,
Entered the court hall and
Sat on the right side.
Arza and food were extravagantly served.
The white palace buzzed with excitement.
The entire khanate came asking Sanal:
"When you conquer the army of *mangas*,
We beg you to free our prince!"

Sanal promised to help the prince.

Sanal planned to enjoy the comfort
Of the white palace only for a day.
But, pleasing and tempting to merrymaking,
The feasts and drinks lasted for two weeks.
Burul Galzan could wait no longer
And neighed, calling Sanal.
Reprimanded by his horse,
Blushing and shaking from drinking,
Sanal mounted Burul and they galloped away.

Seven times seven—
Forty-nine days have passed.
At the white snow mountaintop,
Sanal stretched the silver reins,
Waved with his black whip,
Flashed with his black eyes,
And examined the surrounding
Lands by four sides:
Between the south and the west,
Kyuder's bronze dome
Lit like a bonfire from afar.
How is Kyuder Khan's palace
Compared with Jangar's Bumba?
Sanal wondered.
The palace did not impress
Sanal as the palace bridge.
Made of pure gold,
the bridge majestically shone,
Stretching across the Shartag Ocean.
Walking back and forth,
Sanal tried to calm down
From a sneaking admiration and fear.

Mounting his horse,
Sanal raced through the Golden Bridge.
Next to Kyuder Khan's black banner,
He fastened the horse's forelegs

With iron hobbles out of the best iron,
Tethered the horse's hind legs
With silver fetter-locks out of the best silver,
And entered the golden *torlok*-tower.
Sanal pushed fourteen jade-silver
Shutter doors,
Ringing five thousand door bells,
And sat on the right side,
Joining the feast.
No one noticed that Sanal was a stranger.
Sanal observed that Kyuder Khan's heroes
Looked stronger than his friends.

When Sanal's throat
Warmed up from drinking,
He got up and slowly walked back and forth.
At last, Sanal stood
In front of the silver throne,
Squeezing his fists in his pockets,
He delivered the message
As Jangar Khan's envoy:
"Kyuder Khan, if you wish peace with Bumba,
Pledge your alliance,
Military service for fifty years,
And taxes for one and thousand years.
Kyuder Khan, if you declare war,
I shall rip your black banner
And deliver it to Jangar with your
Eighty thousand piebald stallions!"
Hero White Star,
The council leader of the Left Wing,
Jumped on his feet,
Pulling his black dagger out:
"I would rather stab him
Than listen to his message!"
Kyuder Khan, known as
Kyuder-Who-Rides-an-Elephant, interrupted:
"Hero White Star,

If I send you as an envoy tomorrow,
You would deliver the same message
On behalf of your khan.
Respect his difficult position,
Listen to his words!"

When White Star returned to his seat,
He asked Sanal:
"I heard that Jangar Khan
Has Hero Scarlet Lion Khongor.
How is the leading Lion among all Lions
In comparison with me?"
"Scarlet Lion Khongor is a red wolf
Attacking ten thousand sheep
And a fierce red wolf
Attacking one hundred thousand sheep.
If one hundred thousand lances
Pierce his body at once,
Lion Khongor would not even move
His foot from pain.
When the army retreats,
He is the last who retreats.
When the army attacks,
He is the first who attacks.
Among seven million warriors,
Scarlet Lion is the jewel for the army.
You are a short stump, in comparison!"
Sanal laughed hysterically,
Slapping his thighs.

Hero Black Gunan
From the Right Wing asked Sanal:
"I heard that Jangar Khan
Has Hero Savar Heavy Arm.
How is Hero Savar in comparison with me?"
Serious Sanal, Bulingir's son,
Turned to the right:
"Poor you,
Should I even answer this question?

A giant among all warriors,
He is a falcon tireless in flights.
Savar Heavy Arm loves
His twelve-blades axe.
Tempered in the flames of fights,
Ready on his mighty shoulder
To swing and whack,
It is eighty and one *meters* in length.
Savar Heavy Arm loves
His chestnut mare Kurung Galzan,
In cost it was equal
To thousand-thousands yurts.
Savar throws anyone off the horse,
So great is the power of his heavy arm."

Hero Pine Star
From the Left Wing asked Sanal:
"I heard that Jangar Khan
Has Hero Serious Sanal.
How is Hero Sanal in comparison with me?"
Sanal no longer could bear these questions.
"I feel sorry, but the option of peace
Was offered to you.
I am Serious Sanal, Bulingir's son.
I must rip your black banner,
Put it in my pocket and bring it home
With your eighty thousand piebald stallions
From the headwaters of eighty rivers.
A million guards will race after me.
One of you will fight with me,
But will be tied to the croup of my horse.
You shall remember Serious Sanal, Bulingir's son!"

Enraged, Kyuder Khan's ten thousand heroes
Ran to capture Sanal.
Sanal pulled Fat Belly's black dagger out,
And fought his way out of the palace
Through fourteen shutter gates.
Outside, he grabbed the black banner,

Ripped and hid it in his pocket.
Mounting Burul Galzan,
He raced over the Golden Bridge
To the headwaters of eighty rivers,
Summoned eighty thousand stallions and
Galloped with the herd to the rising sun,
Kicking the leather stirrups
Seven thousand times silently,
Seven thousand times shouting loudly.

The herd moved fast
Like a storm of thick dust,
As they were envious of the speed of wind,
Frightened by scattered pebbles and rocks,
Anxious to touch the ashes of earth.
Ten thousand stallions
Sped against the wind;
The wind played with their manes
And tails like strings on a harp.
Khan Kyuder mounted his Yellow Tsokhor,
As large as a mountain
With a short-cut tail,
And galloped to the east.
Ten thousand boars-heroes and
A million warriors followed the Khan.
The army raced without a stop,
Losing count night after night,
Losing time day after day.

Seven times seven—
Forty-nine days have passed.
At last, they caught up with Sanal.
Hero White Star,
Pulling the reins to the right,
Bowed to Kyuder Khan's left stirrup
And said:
"In difficult times,
You shared with me
Your food from the same plate;

You shared with me
Your clothes that still have your smell.
Grant me permission to fight
Hero Sanal first!"
"Agreed," Kyuder Zan said.
Hero White Star raced toward Sanal.
White Star, while riding,
Stood on the stirrups
And hit Sanal's back with his axe.
Breaking seventy-two hooks of armor,
The blade stuck in Sanal's back muscles.
Sanal lost his consciousness for four days.
White Star grabbed Sanal's armor-vest,
Trying to pull him down to the ground.
But Burul Galzan,
Listening to his rider's knees,
Did not let him fall off the saddle.
The horse kept wounded Sanal
On his back for four days
Until Sanal regained his consciousness.

Hero Sanal pulled the golden reins
And prayed to the sacred protector.
Drawing his axe out,
Sanal hit White Star's back with his axe.
The blade shattered
White Star's eight giant vertebrae,
Crushed his massive ribs,
Disabled the Tangut mind,
Clouded five perceptions,
And damaged the optic nerve
Of his black eyes.
White Star's body fell
On his horse's soft mane.
Sanal pulled White Star's
Coat hem from the back,
Pushed him on Burul Galzan's croup,
Wide as an anvil,

And tying his arms
And legs with the straps,
Secured him to the saddlebow.
Sanal took White Star's horse,
Fixed the empty saddle
Under the horse belly,[2]
And led his horse to the herd.
Driving the herd, Sanal galloped away.

Soon, he covered the distance
Of a three-month journey.
Looking over his shoulder,
Sanal saw Hero Pine Star,
Who was approaching him fast.
I almost died before,
When I let the challenger hit me first,
Sanal thought, turning his horse around.
He hit Pine Star
And drove his horse with the herd.
Enraged Kyuder Khan
Raced toward Sanal on his Yellow Tsokhor,
As large as a mountain
With a short-cut tail.
Chasing Sanal, Kyuder Khan caught
Burul Galzan's sacred tail,
Majestic like a canopy above the croup,
Eighty-eight meters in length.
A million soldiers surrounded Sanal.
Kyuder Khan, releasing the tail, ordered:
"Capture the enemy!"
Five thousand spears
Pierced Burul Galzan's chest.
Five thousand spears
Pierced Sanal's back.

Sanal ground his wisdom teeth,
His twelve courages boiled inside.

2. An empty saddle under the horse belly is a sign of defeat.

He roared: "For Great Jangar! Hurrah!"
Burul Galzan from the loud sound
Jumped in the air eighteen thousand times,
Landed on the ground
Eighteen thousand times.
Five thousand spears broke
And fell from Burul Galzan's chest.
Five thousand spears broke
And fell from Sanal's shoulder blades.
Sanal on his stunning horse galloped away,
Leaving behind his enemies in reverence:
"What a true hero is Jangar Khan's envoy!"

Sanal grew exhausted from the long ride.
The steppe wind covered his face with dust.
The steppe heat burnt his skin on the back.
The warrior-horse exhausted
From the long ride,
The marrow dried in his bones,
The fat melted in his chest.
Burul Galzan fell on the ground,
Crushing dry roots with his chin.
Sanal collapsed next to
His friend's hooves,
Sobbing with tears as clear as *arshan*:
"In the land with neither grass to pinch
Nor water to sip,
Why do you leave me alone
Against the enemies?
Bring me to the Bumba's border,
To the White Tsokolgan Mountain.
It would take you a day at most
And a half at least."
Burul Galzan's ears,
Six *tyo*[3] wide, pricked up;
Scissor-shaped,

---

3. *Tyo*: a measure of the distance between the toe and the ring fingers.

Their tips met in the middle:
"Come here, let's go!"
Sanal mounted his horse in the morning
And arrived at the mountain slope
In the evening.
Burul Galzan, bending his legs, crashed.
Sanal freed eighty thousand
Black stallions to graze
In the velvet of grasslands
And dropped Hero White Star on the ground.
Sanal carried Burul Galzan
On his shoulders to the mountaintop
And hid his dear friend in the cave.
When he descended,
Kyuder Khan was waiting for him.
Sanal clashed with the army of *mangas*.

After fighting for seven days,
Sanal took his sacred amulet off his neck,
Raised it to his forehead,
And looking to the east,
Cried with tears as clear as *arshan:*
"Jangar Khan, why has Golden Heart Shaman
Not spoken to you yet?"
At that time, Jangar's heroes enjoyed
Drinking *arza* and *horza*
And the multi-tiered palace
Buzzed with excitement.
Suddenly, Shaman Golden Heart
Stood forward, calling:
"Our brother Sanal completed his mission
In the foreign country,
He is fighting with the army
Alone at the Bumba border."
Six thousand and twelve boars-heroes
Ran outside, pushing the jade-silver gates,
Mounted their ready horses.
Riding Aranzal,

Jangar Khan led his warriors.
His famous horse-breeder Bor Mangna,
Who is in charge of the court of the khanate stud,
Held the Bumba yellow-golden banner,
The banner gloriously floated on the wind.
Jangar with his six thousand
and twelve boars galloped away.

Savar Heavy Arm could hardly control
His chestnut mare Kurung Galzan.
Pulling the reins to the right,
He bowed to Jangar Khan's left stirrup:
"Jangar Khan, allow me to race first
To the White Tsokolgan Mountain."
"Agreed," replied Jangar.
As Savar barely touched his chestnut mare
With the silver-bronze stirrups,
Kurung Galzan flew,
Covering five *beeria* in one jump.
Red dust fell behind her hooves,
Forming the horizon
That holds the Blue Sky.
From afar, Sanal recognized
This particular trait of his friend's mare.
Sanal thought: I know Savar too well.
After we finish the battle
And return to Bumba,
Warmed up from drinking *arza* and *araka*,
He would brag:
"When you were fighting at the border Tsok,
On the White Tsokolgan Mountain,
I hurried alone to save your life."
Sanal ferociously raced toward the enemy,
Swinging and smashing with his sword—
The heads of five thousand *mangas*
Flew left and right.
Savar Heavy Arm arrived, greeting him:
"My friend Sanal, come here!

Let's embrace each other!
These sheep would not run away from us."
Two heroes dismounted.
Embracing each other, they cried,
Sharing their sad and happy news.

Soon Jangar with six thousand
And twelve heroes arrived.
Seven times seven—forty-nine days,
Jangar's heroes fought against
A million mounted warriors.
They captured, tying one by one,
Kyuder Khan's ten thousand white heroes.
Jangar Khan took his lance
And fiercely attacked Kyuder Khan,
Who was at the center,
Surrounded by his army.
Raising Kyuder Khan
On the tip of his lance,
He brought Kyuder to his loyal
Six thousand and twelve heroes.
Savar Heavy Arm made a gallant canter
On mare Kurung Galzan
And slapped Kyuder Khan
With the stamped declaration of surrender:
"Under the order of the Great Khan Jangar,
You are the subject of Bumba!"
Kyuder Khan bowed
To Jangar Khan three times,
And pledged his alliance,
Military service for fifty years,
and taxes for one and thousand years.
Sanal reminded:
"When you return home, let the prince
From a small island Tib free!"

Jangar and his boars-warriors
Mounted their warrior-horses.
Rattling with their armor,

They raced without a stop to Bumba,
Losing count night after night.
When they reached
The bright-yellow Bumba Tower,
Strong guardsmen opened
The jade-silver gate.
Beaming with the rays of moonlight,
Jangar sat on the throne,
Handsome as a full Moon
On the fifteenth night.
Six thousand and twelve heroes
Sat in seven circles.
Milk from the wild steppe mares
Formed overflowing rivers,
Arza from the wild mares
Formed overflowing lakes.
Pleasing and tempting to merrymaking.
The feasts lasted long.
The drinking lasted long.
When the knights' throats, at last,
Warmed up from drinking,
The multi-tiered palace
Buzzed with excitement.

How Savar Heavy Arm Defeated Kilgan Khan

Six thousand and twelve heroes,
Scions of legendary families,
Sat in seven circles in the court hall.
Milk from the wild steppe mares
Formed overflowing rivers,
Arza from the wild mares
Formed overflowing lakes.
When the multi-tiered palace
Buzzed with excitement,
From the midday sun side,
Chancellor Budin Ulan
Arrived on his black stallion Ut Khar.
He was an envoy from Fierce Kilgan Khan.
Next to the Bumba yellow banner,
Ulan fastened the horse's forelegs
With iron hobbles out of the best iron,
Tethered the horse's hind legs with silver
Fetter-locks out of the best silver,
And entered the golden *torlok*-tower.
Pushing the jade-silver shutter doors,
Ringing five thousand door bells,
He sat on the right side
And joined the feast.
No one noticed that Ulan was a stranger.

When Ulan's throat warmed up from drinking,
He got up and slowly walked back and forth.
At last, Budin Ulan,
Whose warrior-horse is Ut Khar,
Stood in front of the silver throne
With forty-four legs
And delivered the message
As Kilgan Khan's envoy:
"Great Khan Jangar,
I heard that khans
From the four sides of the world
Offered you their daughters to marry,
You did not want to listen to them,
With nothing they withdrew away:
You married Nom Tegis Khan's daughter,
Sixteen-year-old Princess Shavdal.
Give me Shavdal!
I heard that you
Have sorrel stallion Aranzal,
Who was foaled by a five-year-old mare
From the special breed *tundjur*.
Give me Aranzal!
I heard that you have Mingian,
Erke Tug Khan's son.
His inner ocean
Emanates the groundswells of poise,
His inner sun
Emanates the magnetic power.
Give me Mingian!
If you refuse to deliver them,
My seventy thousand army
Shall invade Bumba.
Now, give me the message,
I must return!"

The leading Lion among all Lions,
Scarlet Lion Khongor,
In charge of the Right Wing said:

"If Great Khan Jangar,
The only scion from the ancient
Familial dynasty Tak Zula,
The only grandson of Tangsyk-Bumba Khan,
The only son of Great Uzyunga Khan,
Surrenders in good health,
The lineage and name
Will be forever tarnished.
I, Scarlet Lion Khongor,
Give you a message:
'If my dry body is lost,
Earth will benefit from a handful of ashes!
If my wounded body is lost,
Earth will benefit from a bowl of blood!'"
"Khongor, you shall be sorry
For your words!" Ulan murmured.
Pushing the jade-silver shutter gates,
He ran outside,
Mounted his horse
Next to the Bumba yellow banner and
Galloped toward the midday sun.

Jangar shared his thoughts:
"At my home, when we sit together,
Enjoying drinking *arza,* we are all equal.
But when a stranger came,
Six thousand and twelve boars sat silently.
Only Khongor was strong enough to respond."
From the Right Wing,
Savar Heavy Arm replied:
"My Great Jangar,
When the enemy heard about Savar Heavy Arm,
Many wars were avoided in Bumba.
Why do you value
Scarlet Lion Khongor above us all?
I will leave you,
Move to three Shargul khans,
And return with them to attack Bumba.

Then, you will value my role!"
Savar drank from a yellow porcelain bowl,
Turning it over three times,
Seventy men hardly could raise it together.
His heated heart exhilarated,
Boiling twelve courages inside,
Ready to break out of his chest cage.
His ten fingers
Squeezed into menacing fists.
Savar Heavy Arm roared:
"Bring me my chestnut mare Kurung Galzan!"

A devoted horse-breeder mounted Kurung,
And made an honorable canter
Around the palace.
He fastened the horse's slender forelegs
With iron hobbles out of the best iron,
And tethered the hind legs with silver
Fetter-locks out of the best silver.
He pulled the horse
With fifty *saaids*' sons,
And brought Kurung to the front gate.
On a saddletree panel,
Decorated with silver plaques,
Over a six-layered saddle blanket,
As spacious as a steppe,
He placed a saddle,
As large as an anvil.
Wide and comfortable,
It looked like a canyon.
The saddle was covered with a pillow
Adorned with Tibetan silver.
Along the patterned fenders,
Between the horse's prolonged ribs,
Through the eighty fine silver rings,
The horse-breeder pulled
The leather straps.
When he fastened the girds so firmly,

Sweat and lather released
From the eighty fine silver rings.
When he secured the straps so tight,
The horse's belly tightened
Seventy-two layers of fat.
Chestnut mare played
With the moon and the sun,
Catching their rays
In her thick velvet mane.
She rattled her armor,
Imagining that her four hooves
Were tramping the enemy's land.
The chestnut mare leaped
Upward and forward,
Throwing *saaids'* sons to one corner,
Throwing *saaids'* sons to the other corner.

Savar put on three types of unique battle armor.
He grasped a whip in his grip.
The core was plaited
With three-year-old bull leather,
The surface was made
Of four-year-old bull hide.
Designed as patterns
On the back of a snake,
Boiled in the saliva of a snake,
Soaked in the poison of a snake—
The treated whip
Was famous for its strength.
A steel plate was at the end of the whip;
When it whips, it burns like fire.
A sandalwood handle had, at its end,
A wrist loop made of scarlet red silk.
"You will learn to value me
when I leave!" Savar said.
He walked pressing the coral path
With his red soft leather boots,
Pushing the jade-silver shutter doors,

Ringing the door bells,
He went outside the palace.
Savar mounted his horse,
Hardly touching the stirrup;
The toe of his blood-red
Fine-leather boot moved
As swift as a ruby coal bouncing off fire.
Savar moved traditionally clockwise
From left to right and galloped away.

Kurung Galzan flew faster
Than a blowing wind.
Throwing his rider off the saddle,
Front and back.
Freeing himself from the grip
Of the golden reins.

Seven times seven—forty-nine days,
The chestnut mare raced without a stop.
Savar slowed down
At the observation post—Bolzatin Boro,
Flashing with his black eyes, he examined
The surrounding lands by four sides:
The palace city of Shargul khans
Lit like a bonfire from afar.
Savar galloped toward the palace.

Around one hundred thousand temples
He made a gallant canter,
Traditionally from left to right.
Savar dismounted
In front of the middle palace,
Tying his horse to the saddlebow.
He walked through the hallways,
Pushing fourteen shutter doors,
And entered the golden *torlok* court hall.
Sitting on the right side,
Savar greeted three Sharguls,
Asking about their health.

Without a reply,
Three khans and their *saaids,*
In the feast of the feast,
Drank *arza* for forty-nine merry days.

At last, the eldest Shargul asked:
"What is the reason for your visit?"
"I was disrespected in Jangar Khanate.
I would like to join your army
To conquer Bumba," Savar said.
Three Sharguls decided:
"Without Hero Savar Heavy Arm,
Without Hero-Horse Kurung Galzan,
We will definitely defeat
Jangar's twelve boars.
Let's charge tomorrow,
at the sun's midday!"

A foreigner in Shargul's land,
Savar set up his tent
And dozed through his worries.
In the middle of the night,
He woke up from a vexing noise
In the right corner:
Kurung Galzan was rubbing her muzzle against the tent.
Savar threw over his shoulders an extravagant black fur coat,
Made of soft foal fur, and ran outside.

His mare Kurung Galzan called him
To listen to Jangar's crying song:
"My dear friend Savar Heavy Arm,
After you left, Kilgan Khan's
Seven hundred thousand army invaded Bumba.
In such difficult times,
You were a soaring eagle
Tireless in flights.
You were an attacking falcon
Tireless in fights.
My dear friend, feeling indignity, left me,

Because of mere misunderstanding."
The melody vibrated in the air
On the high note *jingir-jingir*
Three more times,
On the lower note *gunger-gunger*
Three more times.
Savar and Kurung listened to
Jangar's song through the end:
"If my human falcon
Savar Heavy Arm were with me,
I would not be a captive now."
Mare Kurung Galzan said:
"This is why I woke you up."
Savar Heavy Arm saddled his mare,
Wrote a letter to Sharguls,
Explaining his leave,
And left the letter on his bed.

Mounting his horse,
Savar galloped away,
Kicking the bright-yellow stirrups
One thousand times.
The mare rushed,
As if she was scared like a white hare
Jumping out of the sedges.
The mare raced,
As if she was frightened by the whistling
Bullets of pebbles and rocks.
Kurung Galzan threw her rider off
The saddle, front and back,
And left a trail behind of hoof prints
As deep as wells.
The distance of forty-nine days,
Kurung covered within seven days.
In Bumba, only three heroes remained free:
Handsome Mingian, Shaman Golden Heart,
And Gyuzan Fat Belly.
The rest were captured and locked in Kilgan's Khanate.

Savar Heavy Arm mounted his horse
And alone advanced toward
Kilgan Khan's army.
He fought for seven days
Until Kurung's legs became weak.
Savar retreated,
Galloping to Lion Mountain,
Where he greeted his three friends.
Turning the golden reins to the right,
Savar charged toward the army.
The battle lasted for two weeks.
Then, he, steering the reins,
Withdrew and charged again.
Savar Heavy Arm,
Swinging and smashing
With his yellow steel sword,
Ferociously raced to Kilgan Khan,
Who was at the center
Surrounded by his black army.
When he reached Kilgan Khan,
Savar raised his axe
With twelve blades above his head,
And hit Kilgan with one powerful thrust,
Crushing Kilgan's strong ribs
And eight vertebrae bones.
Kilgan Khan lost his Tangut consciousness.
Savar's twelve-blades axe was shattered.
A lanyard loop, made of scarlet red silk
And folded eight times,
Cut his pinky through the bone.

Kilgan Khan fell on the ground
In front of his warriors.
Savar pulled Kilgan's coat hem from the back
And pushed him on Kurung's croup,
Wide as an anvil.
Tying his arms and legs
With the blue silk straps,

Savar secured him to the saddlebow
And galloped to Lion Mountain.
Jangar's three boars-heroes
Greeted Savar and asked Kilgan Khan:
"What did you do to
Great Khan Jangar and Jangar's boars?"
"They are hidden in the cave
On the rock mountain," Kilgan replied.

Four heroes raced to the cave
To save near-dead Jangar and his boars.
They called the healing *arshan* to rain
And revived all wounded heroes.
Recovered, six thousand
And twelve heroes assembled.
Kilgan Khan was ordered
To surrender his golden helmet,
Kilgan Khan bowed
To Jangar Khan three times,
Accepted the tulip-red stamp of surrender,
Pledged the subject allegiance
For one and thousand years.
Then, Kilgan Khan and his seven hundred
Thousand army were set free to return home.

Jangar and his boars-warriors,
Mounted their warrior-horses.
Rattling with their armor,
They raced without a stop to Bumba.
When they reached
The bright-yellow Bumba Tower,
Strong guardsmen opened
The jade-silver gate.
Six thousand and twelve heroes
Sat in seven circles.
Milk from the wild steppe mares
Formed overflowing rivers,
Arza from the wild mares
Formed overflowing lakes.

The multi-tiered palace
Buzzed with excitement.
The statehood they created
Was indestructible,
Its glory was uncontrollable,
Rattling beyond its spacious land.
In bliss and peace,
The Bumba Khanate spectacularly shone.

Cycle 10

How Three Sons Captured Mighty Badmin Ulan

Six thousand and twelve heroes,
Scions of legendary families,
Sat in seven circles in the court hall.
Milk from the wild steppe mares
Formed overflowing rivers,
Arza from the wild mares
Formed overflowing lakes.
When the multi-tiered palace
Buzzed with excitement,
Great Khan Jangar shared his thoughts:
"There were the days when
Aranzal was faster than wind,
A spear was not only radiantly bright—
The radiant spear was sharply precise.
Full of youth and energy,
I married Nom Tegis's daughter—
Sixteen-year-old Shavdal.
After three months of our happy marriage,
Before I united my famous boars,
I wandered in the wide open steppe,
Seeking adventures.
From the side of the rising sun,
Hero Badmin Ulan arrived to conquer
Everyone under the sun.

We met for a wrestling combat
And he overpowered me.

"Before taking my life, he said:
'The last three regrets
Of a defeated man shall be granted.'
I asked the victor:
'Only three months have passed,
Since I married my Shavdal.
I wish to enjoy more my happy marriage.
I wish to assemble the union
Of legendary scions.
I wish to consolidate the four governing
Principles with my own hands.'
'Complete you three wishes
And we shall meet again,' Ulan declared.
Now, the statehood we created is indestructible,
Bumba's glory is uncontrollable,
Rattling beyond our spacious land.
Hero Ulan wants to send two envoys to Bumba;
They are invincible.
Before he sends his envoys,
We must capture Hero Ulan.
What do you think,
My dear six thousand and twelve boars?"
Jangar asked.

Shaman Golden Heart,
Who leads the Right Wing, said:
"Bumba's population is dense
As dust and numerous as ants.
In seventy khanates of Bumba,
There must be a young hero
Born to defeat the enemy.
Let's write a poem of blessing
And announce the search for a hero!"
They asked Nobleman Tsagan,
Mount Golden Sharga,
Handsome Mingian's stallion,

And disseminate the message:
"The khanate's statehood
And enlightened principles
Are in danger of destruction.
Is there a young hero
to defend the Bumba Khanate?"
Nobleman Tsagan spread the announcement
For one, two, three weeks.
Seven times seven—
Forty-nine days have passed.
No one responded.
Returning from the northern side,
Nobleman Tsagan made a call for a hero
In the community of thirty smokes,
As he was reciting the message
Twenty boys played
The *shagai* game near him.
A boy with the scarlet lion mane hair
Dropped his *shagai* bones and two bats
And asked Nobleman Tsagan:
"Honorable Knight,
Please repeat your message."
Nobleman Tsagan
Barely looked at him over his shoulder,
But slowed his horse's gait;
It was neither a trot nor a walk or a halt.
He listened to the boy's steps behind.
After two weeks the boy asked:
"Great Knight, take me with you!"
Nobleman Tsagan seemed ambivalent:
"I was asked to bring
A strong contestant against the hero,
Who defeated Great Jangar in his prime age.
I shall return either alone
Or with this young boy."

After three more weeks,
The boy with the scarlet mane said:

"Sharga's back is long and wide
For two people to ride,
But you are greedy to offer me
A seat on the horseback.
Meet me at the jade-silver palace gates!"
Nobleman Tsagan grabbed his right wrist,
Put him on the horseback
And raced to the khanate.
Nobleman Tsagan dismounted
At the jade-silver gates of the bright-yellow palace.
He hesitated to show the boy
To many *saaids* for two days.
The boy with scarlet mane said:
"You brought me to the palace,
I will bring you inside the palace."
He grasped Nobleman's tulip-red sash
And carried him, emerging in the court hall.

From the Left Wing,
Scarlet Lion Khongor jumped forward:
"Oh no, my little Khoshun!"
Scarlet Lion pulled his son's
Right arm toward the exit,
But Khoshun's feet were glued to the floor.
Scarlet Lion looked at his son and cried:
"Great Jangar initiated this adventure.
Take his son Khar Jilgan with you.
Shaman Golden Heart
Foresaw you in his plan.
Take his son Alia Shonhor."
Sobbing, Scarlet Lion Khongor ran outside.

Great Khan Jangar called Khoshun:
"Come here!"
Jangar put the boy on his right lap
And kissed his right cheek.
Jangar put him on his left lap
And kissed his left cheek.
Then he ordered: "Let's select the best horses for three boys!"

After expecting six thousand
And twelve runners,
They selected Jangar's Aranzal.
The second runner they picked was Aksak Ulan;
Shaman Golden Heart's runner
Was well prepared for this mission.
He drank water from many rivers
And explored many foreign pastures.
The third runner was
Handsome Mingian's Sharga.
A half an *ald* faster
Than the speed of thought,
One *ald* faster than the speed of wind,
Golden Sharga was tempered
In the flames of wars.
Three stallions were brought
To the jade-silver gates.
The horsemen fastened the horses' slender forelegs
With iron hobbles out of the best iron,
And tethered the hind legs with silver
Fetter-locks out of the best silver.
On the saddletree panels,
Decorated with silver plaques,
Over the six-layered saddle blankets,
As spacious as a steppe,
They placed the black saddles.
Along the patterned fenders,
Between the prolonged ribs,
Through the eighty fine silver rings,
The horsemen pulled the leather straps.
When they fastened the girds so firmly,
Sweat and lather released
From the eighty fine silver rings.
When they secured the straps so tightly,
The horse bellies tightened
Seventy-two layers of fat.
And in the end, they attached the bells
On the manes and necks.

The three stallions' croups were divine—
The beauty of their power
Was concentrated in their croups.
Sharp precision was
In their expressive eyes,
Rapid speed was in their swift feet.
Their marvelous ears were scissor-shaped,
Their tips were meeting in the middle.
Three stallions played
With the moon and the sun,
Catching their rays
In their thick velvet manes.
They rattled with their armor and imagined
That their hooves tramped the enemy.
Throwing stable men to one corner,
Throwing stable men to the other corner,
Three stallions leaped upward and forward.
Three boys put on their battle armor.
Each grasped a whip in the right hand.
Its core was plaited with three-year-old bull leather,
Its surface was made of four-year-old bull hide.
Resembling patterns on the back of a snake,
Boiled in the saliva of a snake,
Soaked in the poison of a snake—
The treated whip was famous for its strength.
A steel plate was at its end;
When it whips, it burns like fire.
A sandalwood handle had, at its end,
A wrist loop made of scarlet red silk.

After three boys were thoroughly examined,
The decision was made:
"The boys were capable
To accomplish the mission!"
Jangar and six thousand and twelve heroes
Recited a poem of blessing,
Wishing them success in their journey;
Tears, as pure as *arshan,*

Were rolling down their cheeks.
Holding gracefully the silver-bronze reins,
Three boys made a gallant canter
Around the palace,
Bowed to the lamas and galloped away.

Seven times seven—
Forty-nine days have passed.
At the observation post—Bolzatin Boro,
They dismounted,
Tying their horses to the saddlebows.
Shaman Golden Heart followed the boys,
Racing on Savar's mare Kurung Galzan.
A black silk cape over his shoulders
Floated magnificently in the wind.
"My dear boys,
The bones of your arms and legs
Have not hardened yet.
Listen to your uncle.
I came here to show
The path in your adventure.
There will be a vast swamp on your way.
The time to walk
Across the swamp is one life.
The time to walk
Along the swamp is beyond one life.
Aksak Ulan shall safely
Lead you out of this swamp.
After three months,
In the shade of three magic
Sandal and poplar trees,
You shall meet five hundred maiden-witches.
Do not look straight at their eyes!
Golden lassos are hidden
In their delightful mouths.
Behind their divine lips are traps.
Release Aranzal's reins.
Aranzal shall safely

Lead you out of this place.
Three more months will pass.
You will meet a goddess-faced woman,
Strolling along the road.
Sun and Moon compete
With the beauty of her face.
Offering you drinks and delights
With ninety-nine hidden spells,
She will try to lure you, singing:
'My young brothers
Might be thirsty and hungry.'
Golden Sharga shall safely
Lead you out of her trap."
Shaman bade farewell
And headed back to Bumba.

Three boys mounted their horses and
Raced toward the rising sun.
Their horses flew like a blowing wind,
Slightly under the heavy clouds,
Slightly above the feather grass.
A leap of their hind legs
Covered the distance of one day;
A jump of their forelegs
Covered the distance of two days.
When they dived,
Touching the black soil with their chins,
They snorted fire,
Burning the grass into ashes.
Then, they soared like a white hare,
Gently brushing the young grass fields.

At last, they saw the vast swamp.
As Uncle Shaman suggested,
They sent Aksak Ulan first.
The horse drank water from many rivers
And explored many foreign pastures.
Tracing the ten-year-old path
Like a spider,

Tracing the twenty-year-old path
Like a beetle,
Touching the ground barely with his hooves,
The warrior-horse masterfully passed through the swamp.
Two stallions, following Aksak Ulan,
Also crossed the swamp safely.

Three boys galloped without a stop
For three months.
In the shade of three magic
Sandal and poplar trees,
Five hundred witches approached them.
Offering them drinks and delights
With ninety-nine hidden spells,
They lured them, singing:
"Our young brothers might be thirsty and hungry."
Releasing the silver-bronze reins,
The boys let Aranzal go first.
Aranzal, straightening his ears,
Six spans in width,
Jumped in the air eighteen thousand times,
Landed on the ground
Eighteen thousand times.
As if he was frightened
By scattered pebbles
Under his hooves,
Aranzal, evading the maidens,
Galloped away.
The two horses followed Aranzal
And safely escaped.
Five hundred witches cried,
Covering their mouth
From surprise and frustration:
"We lured hundred thousands
Without a combat,
We lured ten thousands
Without a delay.
We failed to catch these young warriors.

Let's wish them to safely
Complete their task."

The boys raced three months without a stop.
Suddenly, they saw a goddess-faced lady.
Sun and Moon compete
With the beauty of her face.
She greeted them,
Asking them to come closer.
They ignored her repeated
Greetings three times.
Then, Khoshun freed Golden Sharga's reins,
Kicking the bright colorful stirrups
Seven thousand times silently,
Seven thousand times shouting loudly.
Altan Sharga jumped in the air
Eighteen thousand times,
Landed on the ground
Eighteen thousand times.
Sharga, evading the maiden, galloped away.
The two horses followed Sharga
And safely escaped.
The lady-witch cried behind:
"How did I miss such fast runners?
How did I miss such heroic boys?"
Excited about their successful start,
The boys raced happily to the rising sun.

When they entered
The desolate black mountain,
Aksak Ulan suddenly
Fell down on the ground.
Three boys dismounted and cried,
Hugging the horse:
"We can neither leave Aksak
Nor stay here long."
They cried over the sick horse
For three weeks.
The next day, Aksak Ulan

Shared his secret thoughts:
"Long time ago,
During Jangar's engagement to Shavdal,
I raced nine *beeria* ahead of Aranzal.
Jangar was so enraged that
He crashed my feet,
Aranzal protected me and saved my life.
I don't take the orders from Jangar,
But because I love Aranzal, I will get up
And join you in your mission."
Three boys mounted their
Horses and galloped away.

Soon they saw the *ole-fluffy white—*
Maikhan Mountain.
The mountain slope for climbing
Was on the southern side.
The boys met an *ole-fluffy white—*
Gyrfalcon on the cliff
And greeted her respectfully.
The gyrfalcon placed her two black chicks
On her *ole*-fluffy white wings.
She sat, facing the sun,
And kept her chicks warm.
The gyrfalcon said:
"In Badmin Ulan's Khanate,
My hatchlings died three times
Over the last three years.
I heard that in Bumba Khanate
The passing of time does not exist,
Death does not enter the place.
I will migrate to Bumba to save my chicks."
The boys asked the bird:
"When you reach Bumba,
Let them know that we have entered
Badmin Ulan Khanate."

Three boys mounted their horses
And raced without a stop.

At last, the Eagle Glass Tower
Lit like a bonfire from afar.
Scarlet Lion Khongor's son
Khoshun Ulan asked his friends:
"How should we capture the *mangas*?
Jangar Khan's son Khar Jilgan proposed:
"I will throw a lasso
At the Eagle Tower and pull it down.
You will catch Badmin Ulan."
Shaman Golden Heart's son
Alia Shonhor proposed:
"Jangar Khan was in his prime age,
When he lost to Badmin Ulan.
We should use clever tricks, not strength."
Scarlet Lion Khongor's son Khoshun said:
"I disagree with Jilgan
And agree with Shonhor."
Three boys collected *za*-shrubs,
Started a campfire
And boiled a sandalwood red tea.
Then they set up a bright-red tent,
In value it was equal
To ten thousand yurts.
In its shade,
Stretching out like three resting belts,
Warming up, pink like a *sukha* flower,
The boys fell into a deep sleep.

Seven times seven,
Forty-nine days have passed.
When they woke up,
They enjoyed a morning tea.
Turning their horses
Into three scrubby colts
And themselves into three filthy boys,
They trotted *dab-dab*
Toward the Eagle palace.
They left their colts

On the shores of the great lake.

Scarlet Lion Khongor's son Khoshun said:
"First, I will examine the palace kitchen."
In the busy palace kitchen,
The chefs prepared an extravagant banquet,
Serving the roasted horsemeat
As a main course,
Made out of nine three-year-old mares.
Khoshun ran inside the kitchen,
Grabbed a roasted leg
From the platter and dashed outside,
As he was chased,
Khoshun gnawed the roast leg,
Spitting out the large chewed
Bones out of his mouth,
Blowing out the tiny
Bones out of his nose.
The head chef brought
The thief to the Khan, saying:
"This devil stole the roast dish
and ate the entire leg,
Spitting out the large chewed
Bones out of his mouth,
Blowing out the tiny
Bones out of his nose."
Khoshun replied:
"Impossible! I am a little filthy boy.
How can I eat the entire leg of a horse?
You fed your big black
Shepherd dog, not me."
The Khan asked his many *saaids*
To resolve the issue.
The *saaids* decided:
"The boy is too weak to carry
And eat the horse leg.
The head chef is responsible for the loss."
Khoshun recited a toast

In honor of Khan Badmin Ulan,
Who sat on the beautiful throne
Above his *saaids*.
Impressed with Khoshun's masterful
Poetic rhetoric,
Khan Ulan announced:
"Be my honorary toast maker,"
Throwing over Khoshun's
Shoulders an elegant cape.
Khoshun asked:
"I shall move my old parents to *tsakhar*.
Please give me a pitcher
Of *araka* and a roast leg."
Khoshun fed his two friends
On the shores of the great lake.
"Tonight, I will enter
The golden *torlok* court hall.
Khar Jilgan, you shall attack
Eighteen thousand outside guards.
Alia Shonhor, you shall attack
Eighteen thousand internal guards.
Bring both your horse and Golden Sharga,"
Khoshun said.

At midnight, Khoshun
Turned himself into a venomous snake.
Bending his spine into serpentine coils,
Khoshun moved fast, passing
Eighteen thousand outside guards,
Eighteen thousand internal guards.
Crawling through the cracks
Of fourteen doors,
Khoshun emerged in the *torlok* court
and sat on the right side of the doorstep.
In the dim light of the high white lantern,
Khan Badmin Ulan slept
On the white sacred throne.
Khoshun went to the left corner

And poured himself a drink.
He drank from a yellow porcelain bowl,
Turning it over seventy-one times,
One and seventy men
Hardly could raise it together.

At last, his heated heart exhilarated,
Boiling twelve courages inside,
Ready to break out of his chest cage.
His ten white fingers
Squeezed into menacing fists.
His sharp black eyes rolled
In the eye sockets twelve times,
Adjusting the vision into
The perception of an attacking falcon.
Khoshun recited:
"If my dry body is lost,
Earth will benefit from a handful of ashes!
If my wounded body is lost,
Earth will benefit from a bowl of blood!"
Khoshun raised his golden-steel sword
Above his body, exclaiming:
"I am not the one who is raising my hand.
Jangar Khan is raising his hand!"
Khoshun stabbed
Badmin Ulan with the sword,
Turning it in his stomach
Seventy-one times.

Badmin Ulan Khan jumped on his feet
and threw Khoshun into the right dungeon.
But clever Khoshun
On the pinky toe of his right foot
Resisted the fall
And jumped back on his feet.
Badmin Ulan threw
Khoshun into the left dungeon.
But clever Khoshun
On the pinky toe of his left foot

Resisted the fall
And jumped back on his feet.
Khoshun, grappling the Khan,
Threw him at the throne with all his might.
Tying Badmin Ulan's hands and feet
Together behind his back,
As wide as an anvil,
Khoshun put him in the yellow sack.
He threw the sack over his shoulder,
Pushed fourteen shutter doors
And ran outside.

Khoshun called Khar Jilgan,
Who battled against
Eighteen thousand internal guards,
And threw the yellow sack with Ulan to Jilgan
Over three hundred thousand heads.
But at that time,
Aranzal soared high and plummeted,
And Khar Jilgan could not catch
The yellow sack with Badmin Ulan
and it fell on the crowd of guards.
Khoshun jumped over
Three hundred thousand heads,
Grabbed the yellow sack,
And threw it back to Khar Jilgan.
But Aranzal nose-dived
and Khar Jilgan dropped the sack.
Khoshun jumped down,
Catched the falling sack,
and threw it back to Jilgan, shouting:
"If Khar Jilgan cannot do it,
Dear Aranzal, you catch
The sack and run away."
With Jilgan on his back and
Ulan inside the sack
Aranzal galloped away.
Khoshun jumping over three thousand heads,

Landed on Golden Sharga's saddle pillow
Adorned with Tibetan silver.
Two boys raced, following Aranzal.
"Let's cover the distance of nine months within nine days,"
    they said.

After five days, Khan Ulan's Hero Samba,
Who rode Black Saaral,
As large as a mountain,
Caught up with the two boys.
Khoshun slowed down:
"My dear Alya Shonhor,
Race on Aksak Ulan ahead!
I on Sharga will fight boar Samba."
Suddenly, Samba riding on Black Saaral
Passed Khoshun and attacked Shonhor.
Drawing his axe out,
Khoshun hit boar Samba's back with his axe.
The blade shattered
Samba's eight giant vertebrae
And crushed his massive ribs.
Hero Samba lost his consciousness.
Closing his black eyes,
He fell on his horse's soft mane.
Khoshun pulled the hem of Samba's
Atlas silk robe,
And tied his arms and legs
With the straps behind his back.
Khoshun, to avert Samba's magic revival,
Cut Samba's body and tossed the remnants
Into the Ganga Ocean.

By that time, Khar Jilgan dismounted Aranzal
At the Bumba jade-silver gates.
Many *saaids* invited Khan Badmin Ulan to sit
On the silver throne on the right side,
But Khan Ulan went straight
To the golden throne and sat above Jangar.
At last, Khongor 's son Khoshun and

Shaman Golden Heart's son Shonhor
Reached Bumba.
The boys made a gallant canter
Around the palace.
Pushing fourteen jade-silver shutter doors,
Ringing five thousand door bells,
They entered the golden *torlok* court hall.
Great Khan Jangar greeted them warmly.
The feast lasted for seven times seven—
Forty-nine days.

Khan Badmin Ulan said:
"Dear Jangar Khan,
There were the days when
Your spear was not only radiantly bright—
The radiant spear was sharply precise.
Your Aranzal was faster than wind and
You were full of youth and energy.
When you lost in the combat, I said:
"Complete your three wishes and
We shall meet again.
Now, we have met.
Keep the statehood
That you have built indestructible.
Keep Bumba's glory
That you have created uncontrollable,
Rattling beyond your spacious land!"
Khan Badmin Ulan
Bade farewell and galloped away.

Six thousand and twelve heroes,
Scions of legendary families,
Sat in seven circles in the court hall.
In bliss and peace,
The Bumba Khanate spectacularly shone.
The people's statehood was strong as a rock.
Their faith of the Buddhas beamed like the sun.
Milk from the wild steppe mares

Formed overflowing rivers,
Arza from the wild mares
Formed overflowing lakes.
Pleasing and tempting to merrymaking.
The feasts lasted long. The drinking lasted long.

GLOSSARY

ald	A measure of length approximately equal to the span between two wide-open arms of an adult.
araka	A fermented milk alcoholic beverage.
arshan	A divine nectar drink for the gods that has purifying and healing powers for humans.
arza	A fermented milk alcoholic beveragethat is twice distilled.
beeria	A measure of length equal to one mile.
Bolzatin Boro	Public towers for observation and shelter along the steppe highway. *Bolza* means "periodically" in terms of time, or "repeatedly" in terms of distance; the posts were built over a certain distance. *Boran* means "storm"; the posts also functioned as storm shelters.
edmeg	A cottage cheese–like substance remaining after distilling a milk alcoholic beverage.
garuda	Eagle.
hermeg	Sour milk remaining after distilling a milk alcoholic beverage.
horza	A fermented milk alcoholic beveragethat is thrice distilled.
jangarchi	Singers of the epic *Jangar*.
khatun	Queen.
magtal	A poetry of admiration, praise, or wishing well. The *magtal* reciting was also a traditional performance in private and

	public banquets. The *magtals* form the building-block passages in *Jangar* (*magtals* for Jangar's horse or Khongor's boots).
mangas	Half-human giants.
saaids	Members of the nobility.
sengche	Chief of the household administration, in charge of ceremonies and staff.
shagai	An astragalus sheep-bone, used for throwing games, board games, and fortune-telling.
sukha	Tavolga (*Filipendula rubra*), also known as Siberian meadowsweet; pink flowers growing in Eastern Siberia, the Far East, and Mongolia.
tamga	A stamp that declares the subject's dependence.
torlok	A round tower with a domed top, located at the center of the palace and serving as a court room, with the formal seat of the Khan; a specific term in Kalmyk architecture meaning "soar high in the sky."
tsakhar	District for servants outside the palace city.
tyo	A measure of the distance between the thumb and the index fingers.
za	Saxaul (*Haloxylon aphyllum* Minkw.), the main arboreal cover in the continental steppes of Central Asia; used as firewood by local nomads.

Founded in 1893,
UNIVERSITY OF CALIFORNIA PRESS
publishes bold, progressive books and journals
on topics in the arts, humanities, social sciences,
and natural sciences—with a focus on social
justice issues—that inspire thought and action
among readers worldwide.

The UC PRESS FOUNDATION
raises funds to uphold the press's vital role
as an independent, nonprofit publisher, and
receives philanthropic support from a wide
range of individuals and institutions—and from
committed readers like you. To learn more, visit
ucpress.edu/supportus.